Alphabet & Numbers
6" x 7"

72 Stained Glass Patterns

Art Deco

   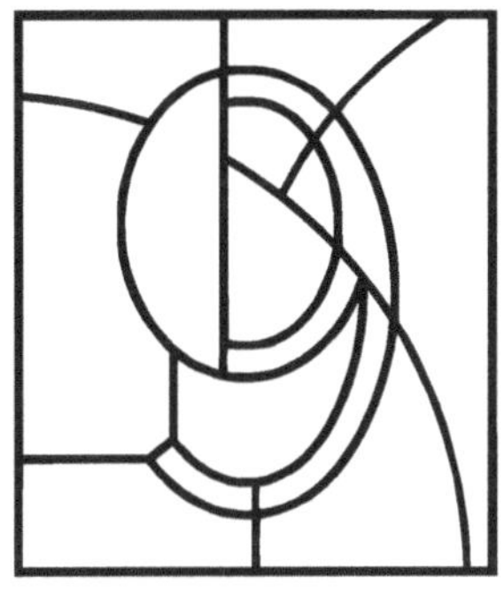

Abstract

 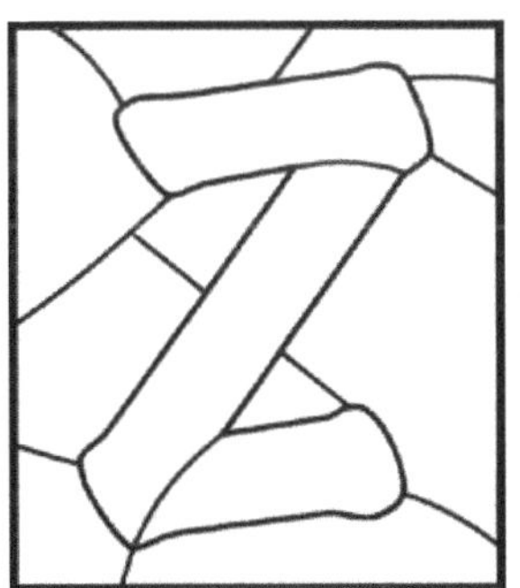 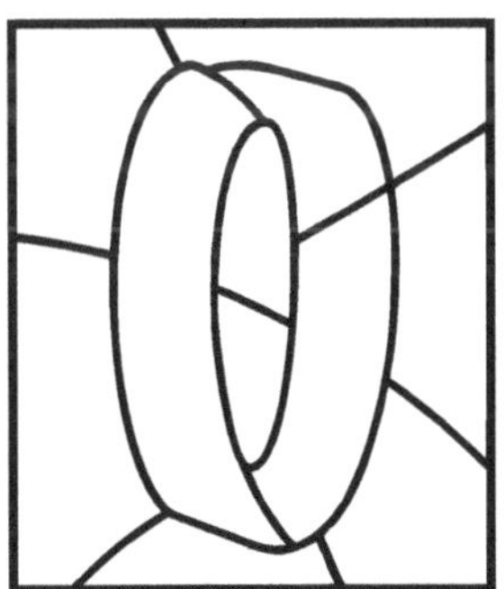 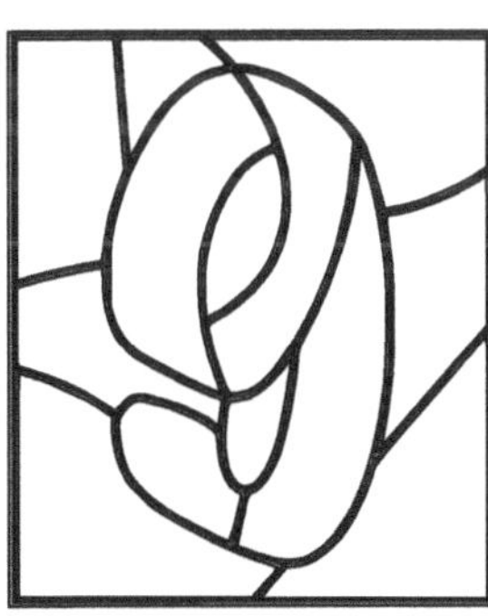

ISBN 979-8-8692-6849-5

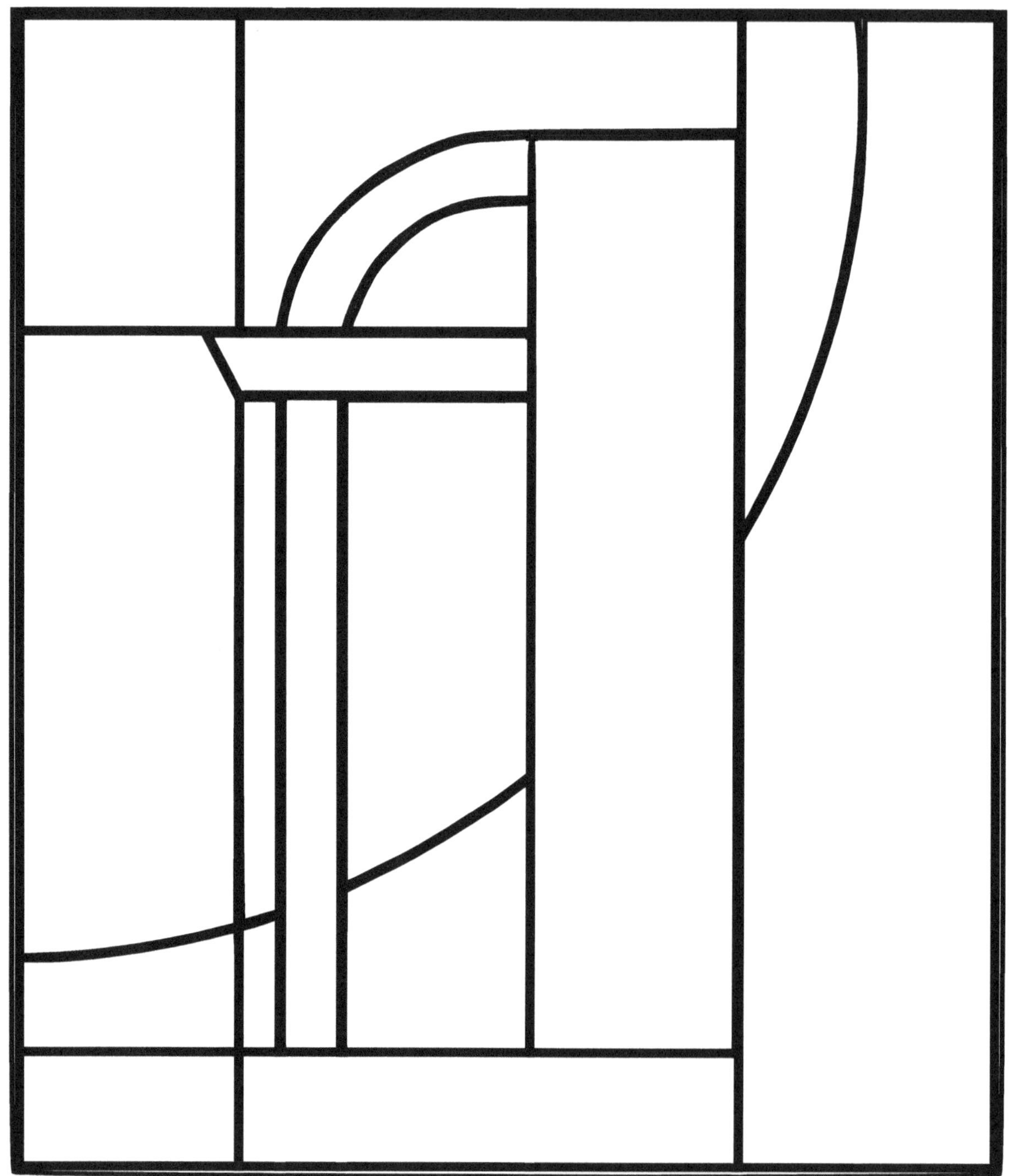

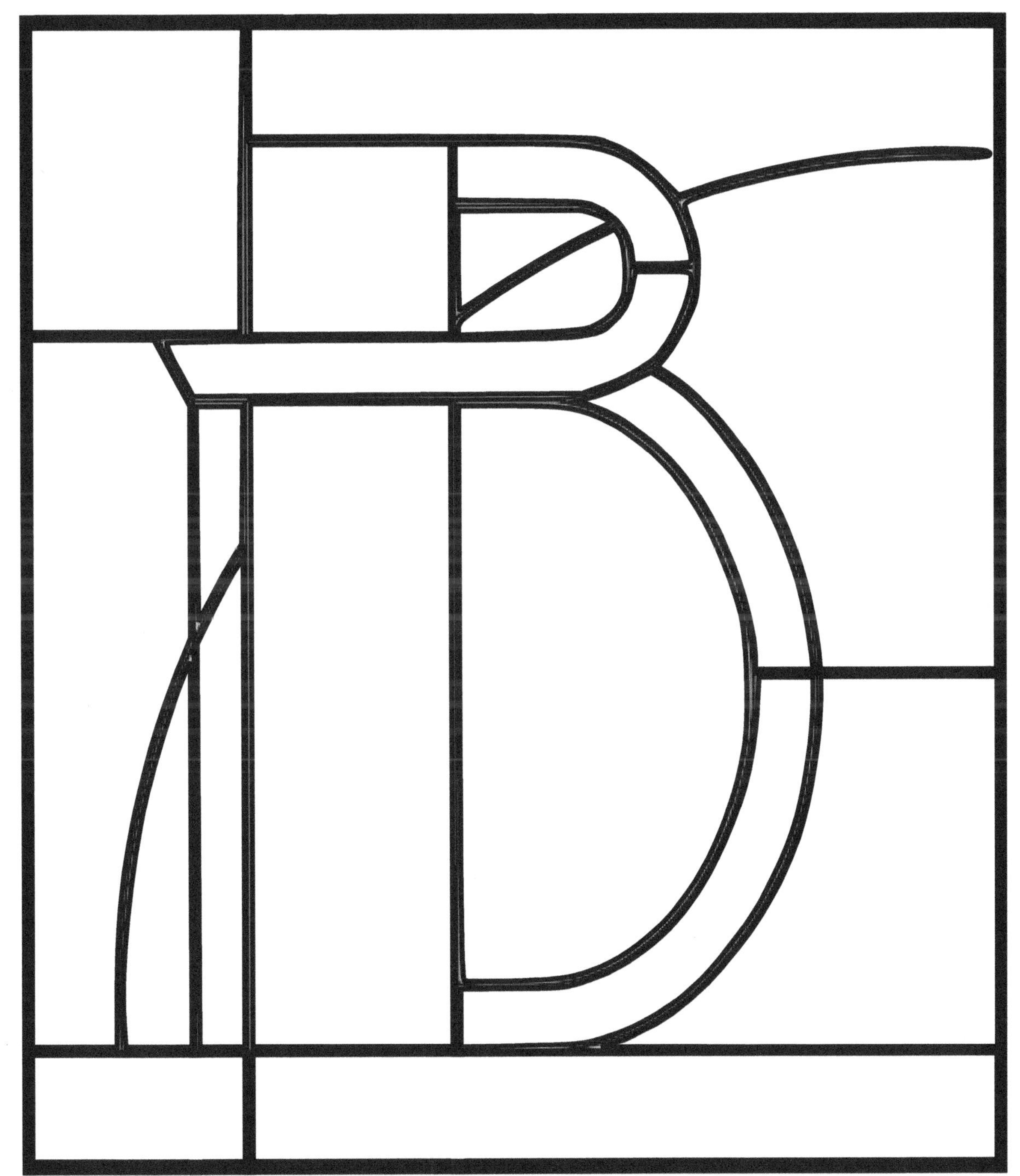

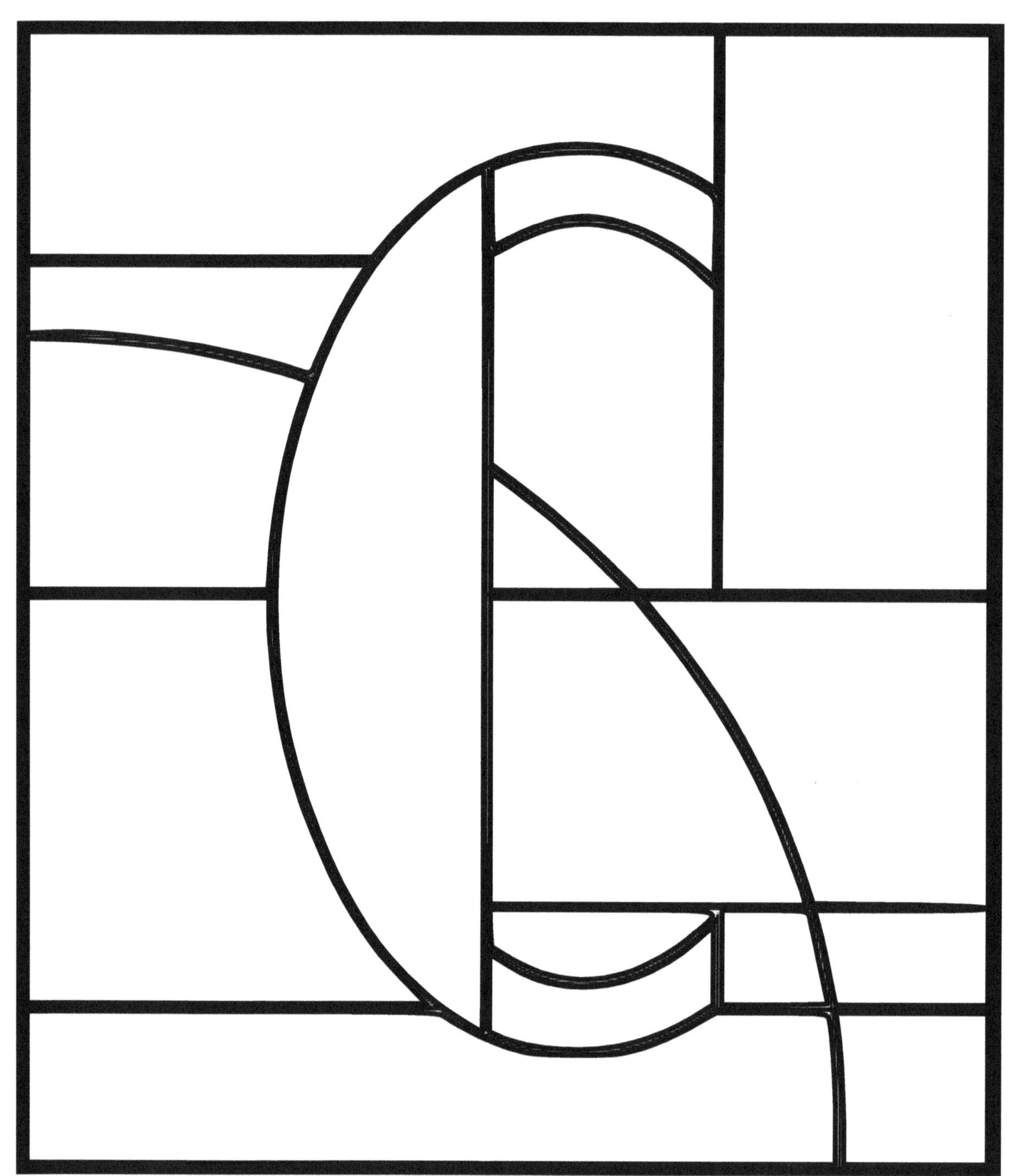

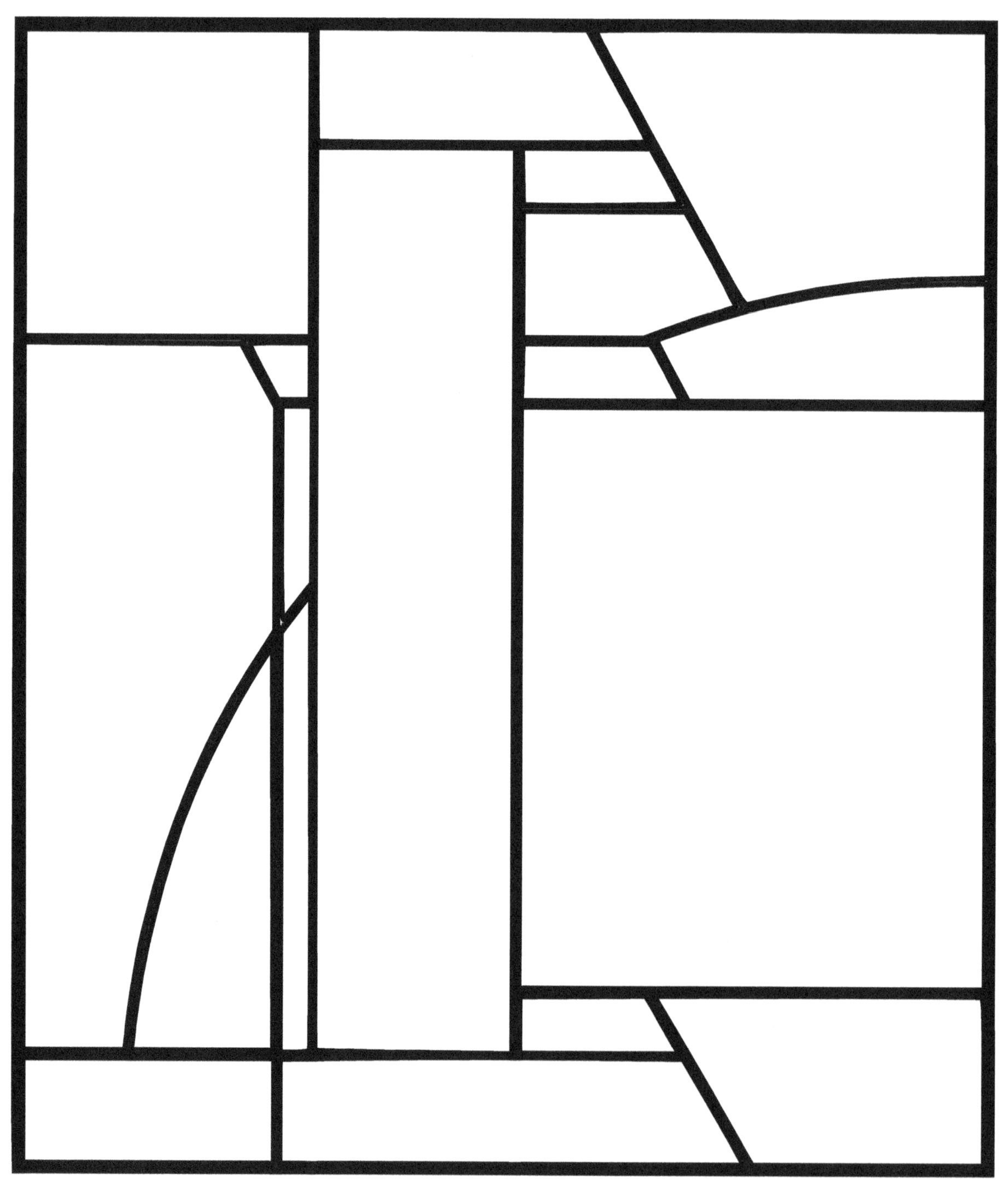

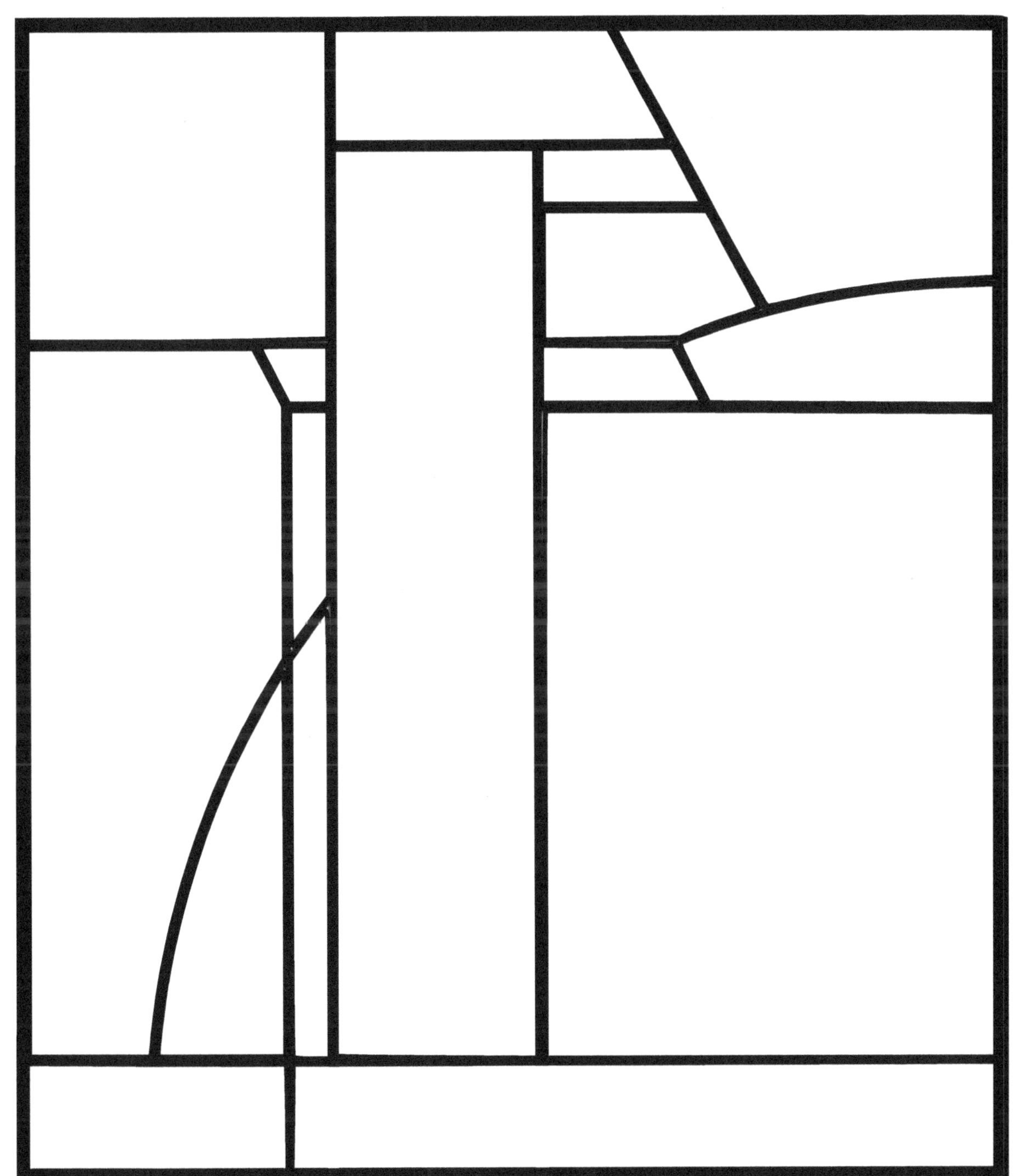

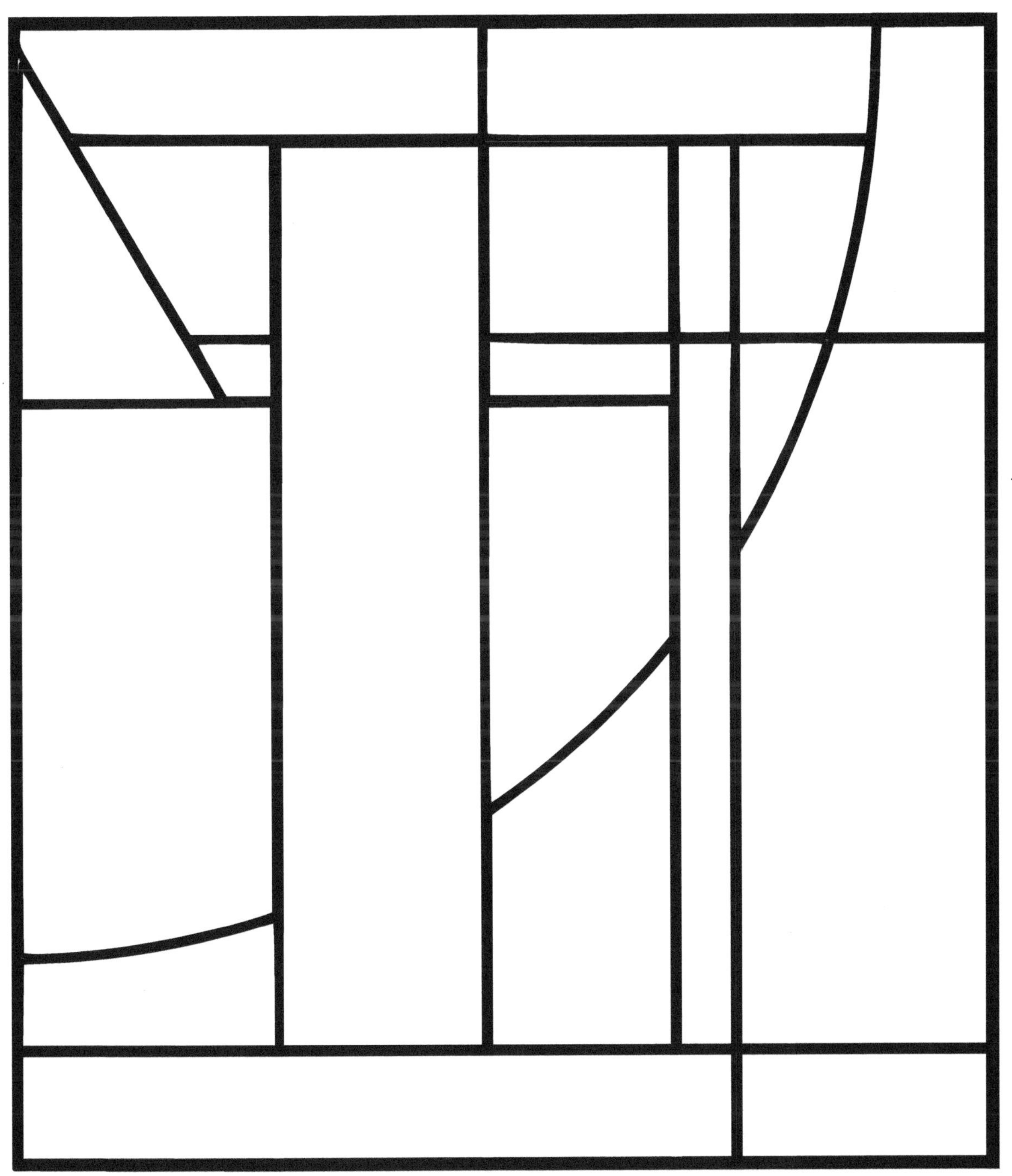

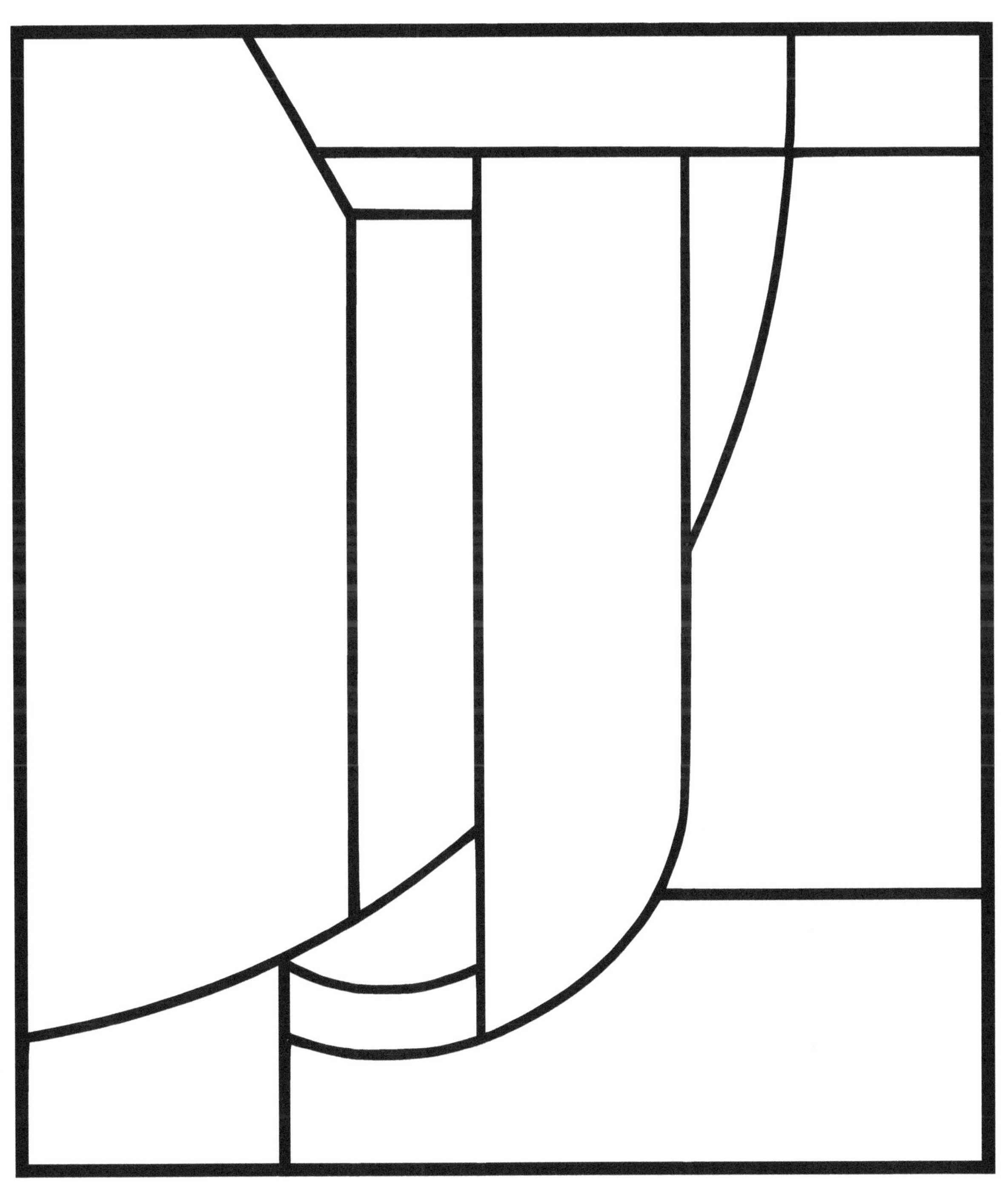

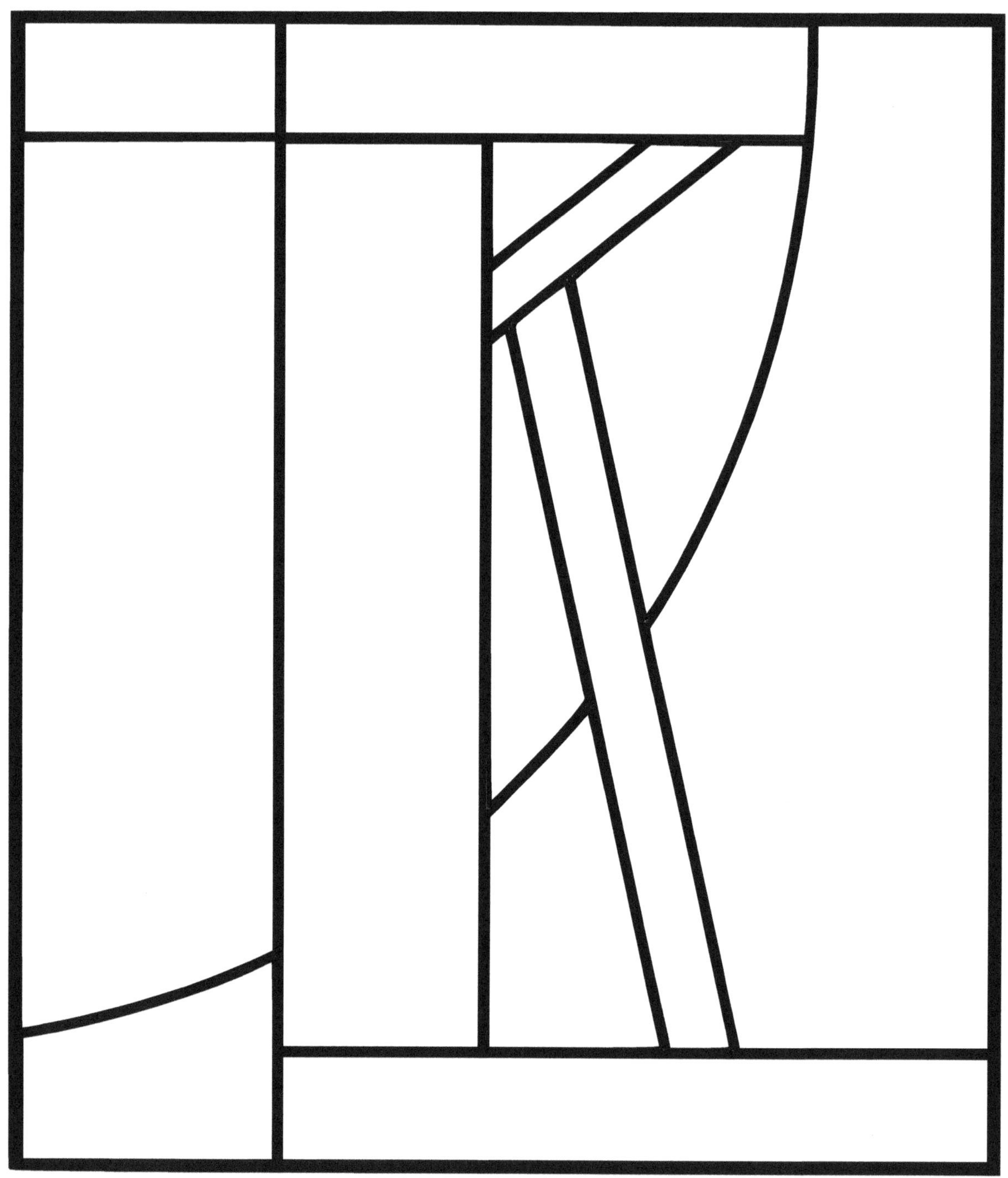

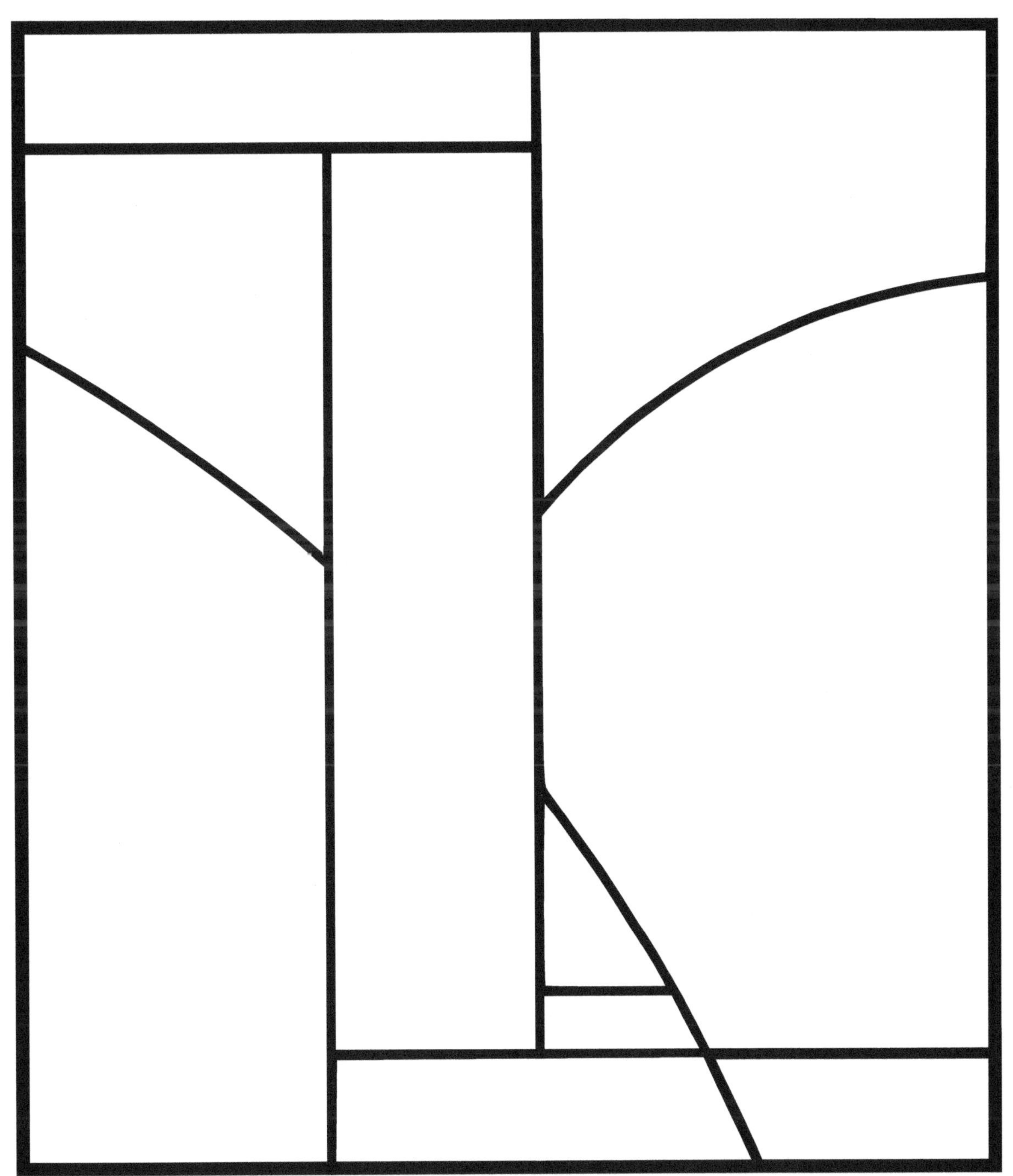

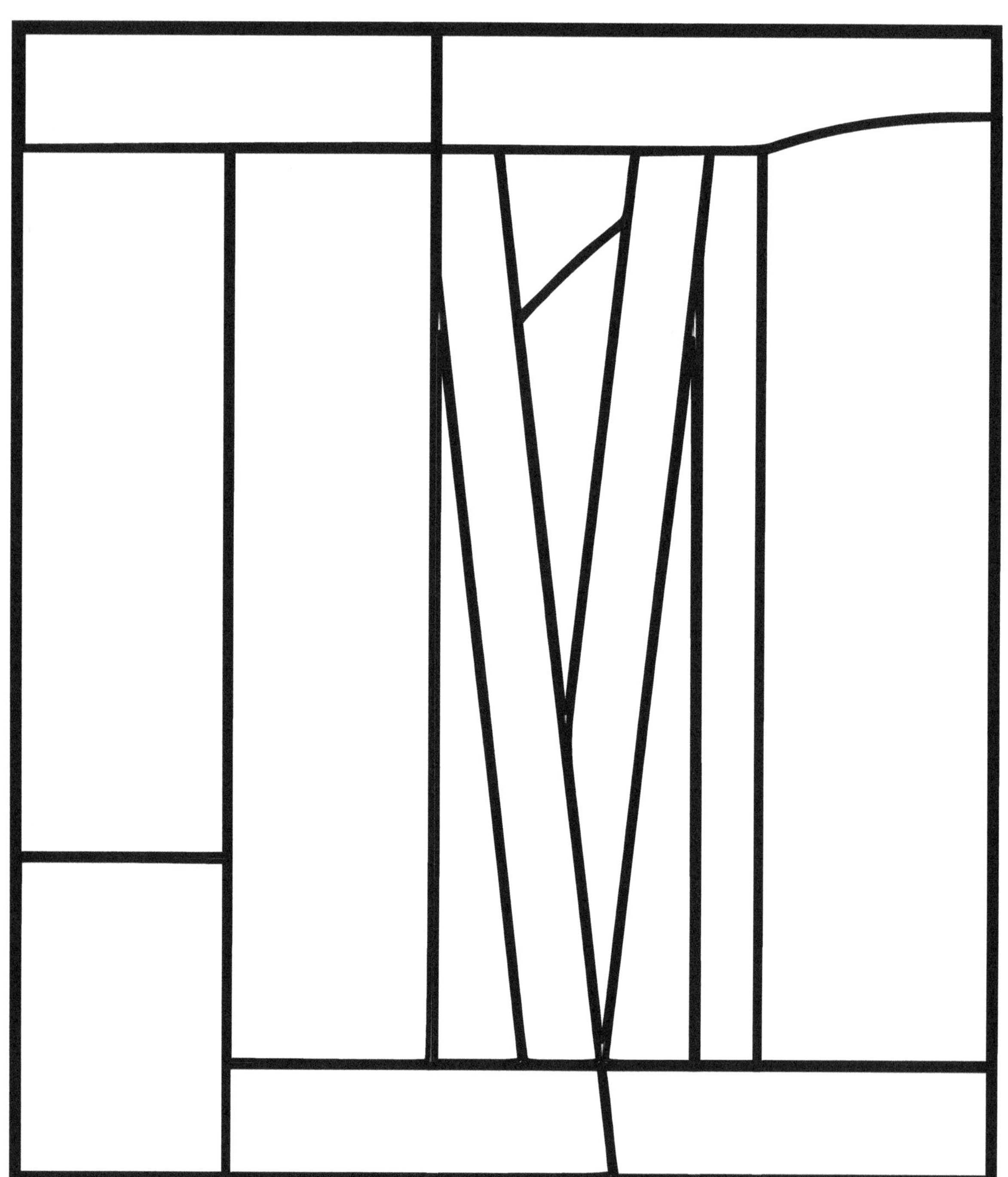

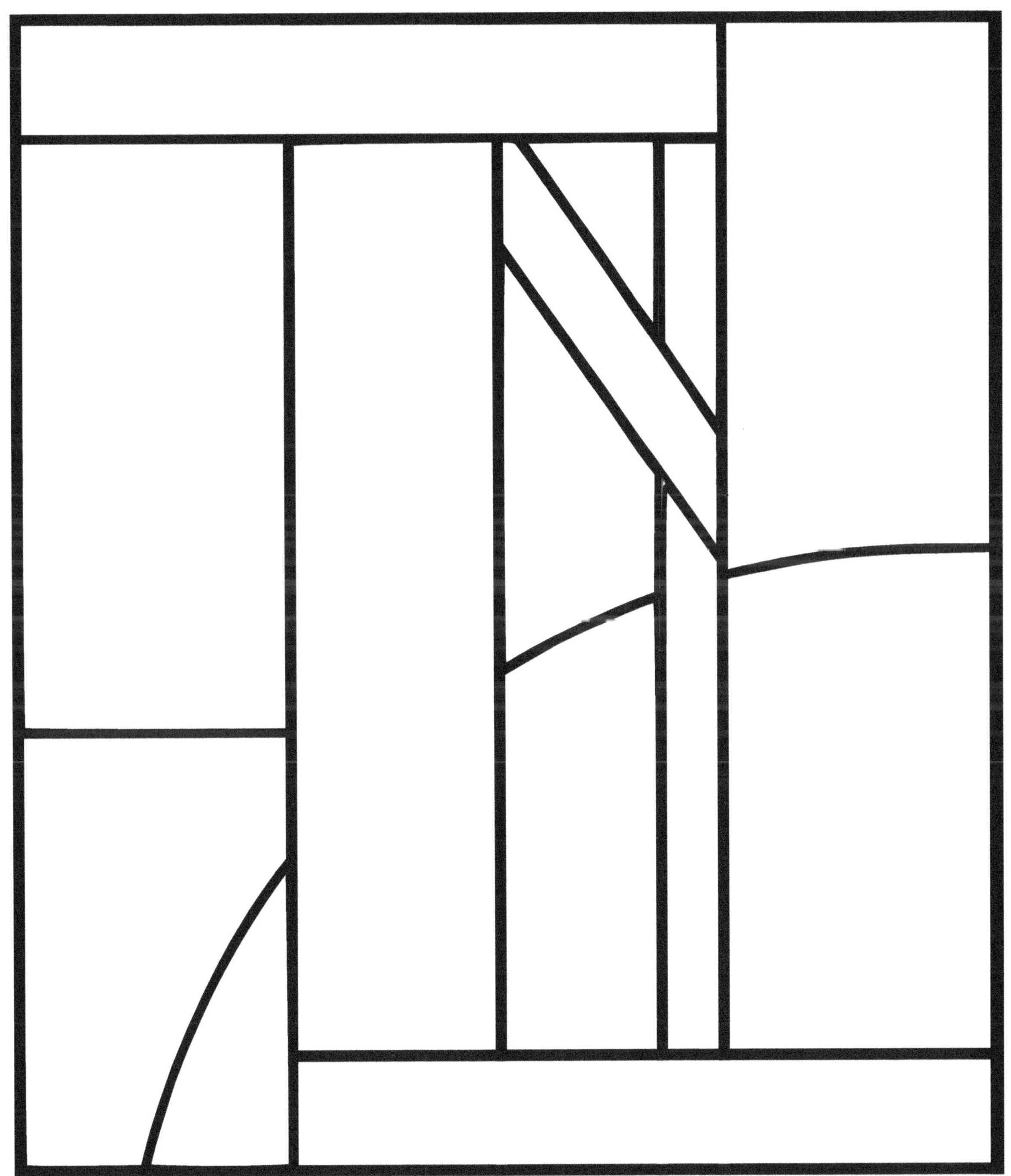

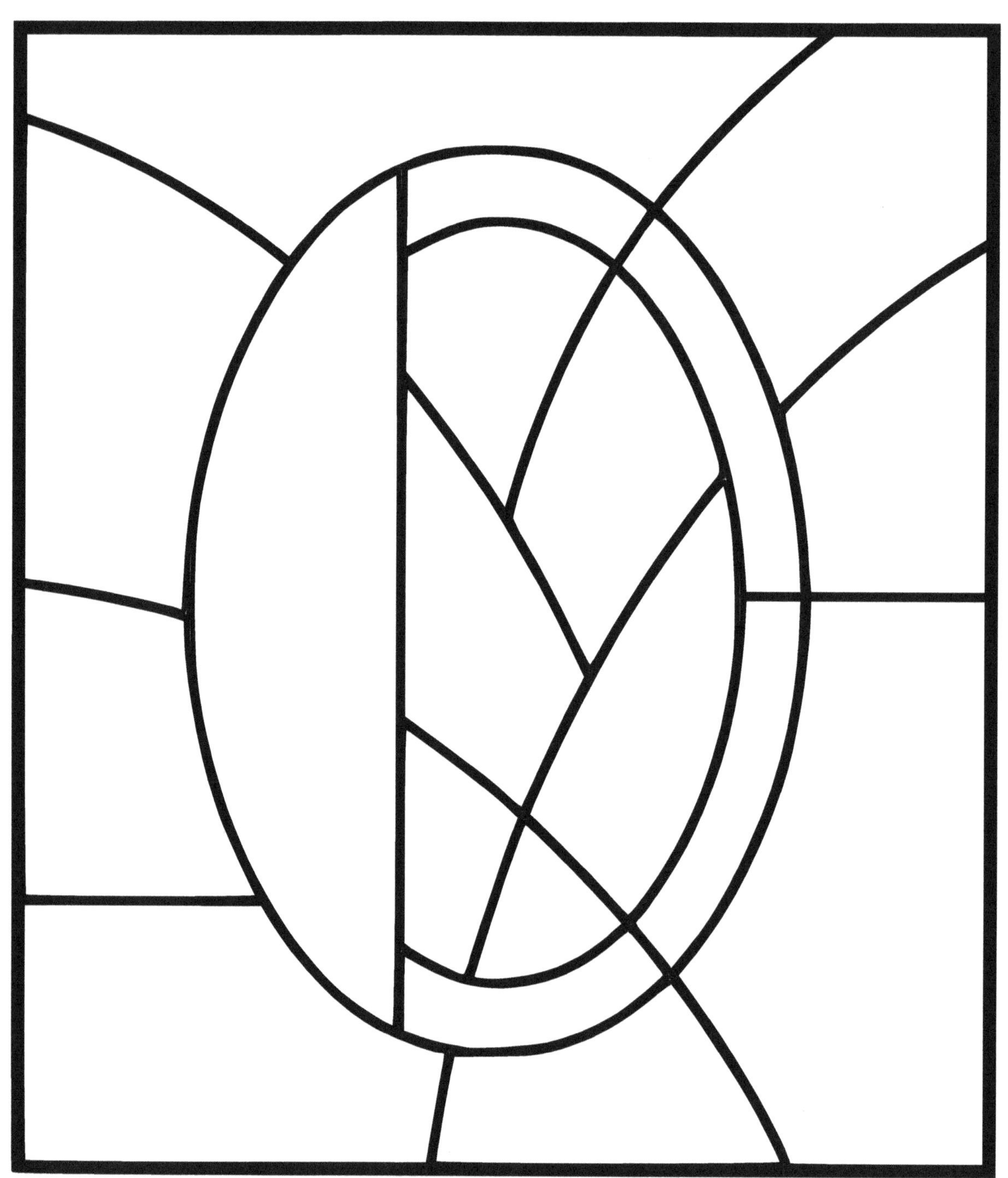

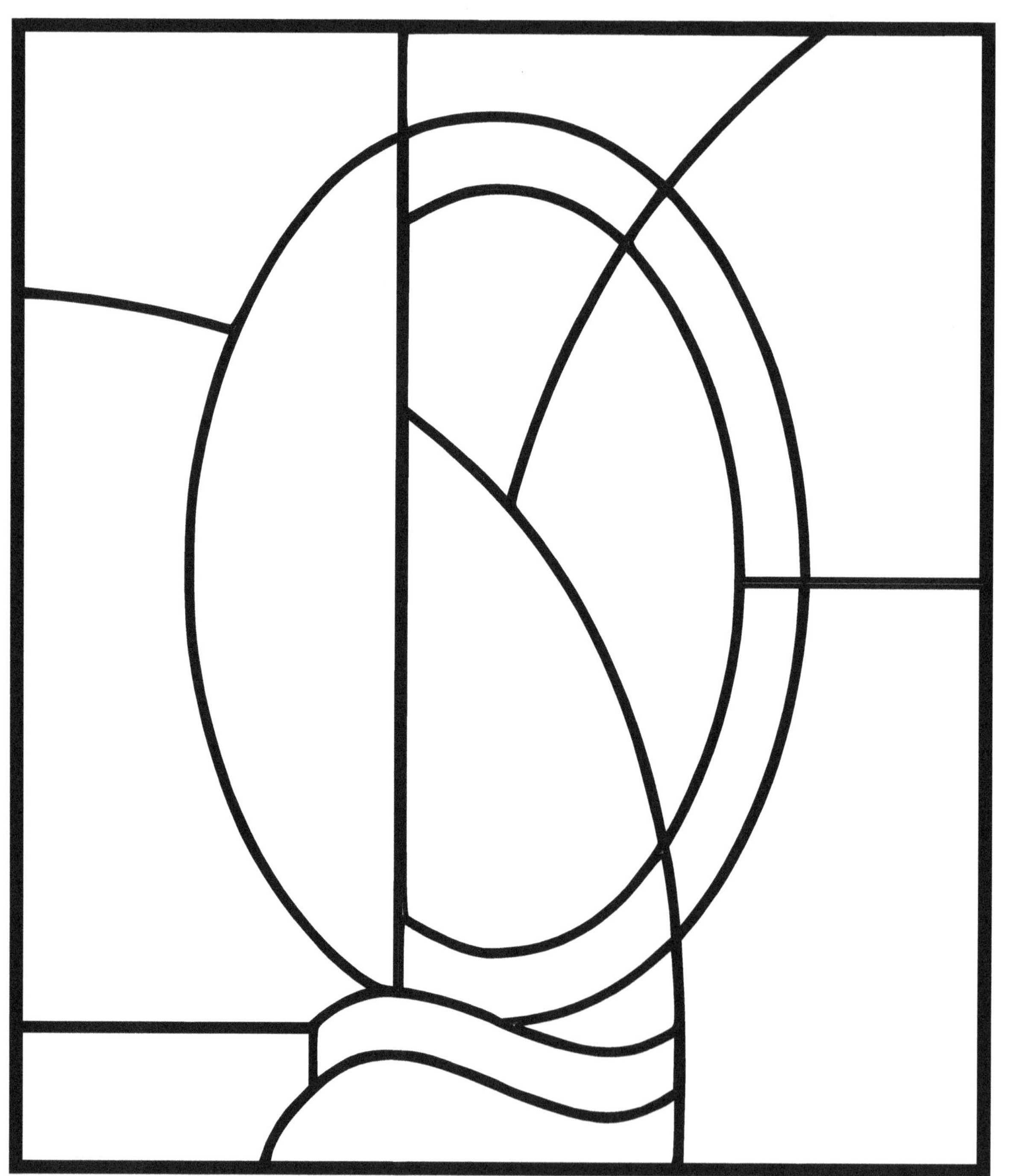

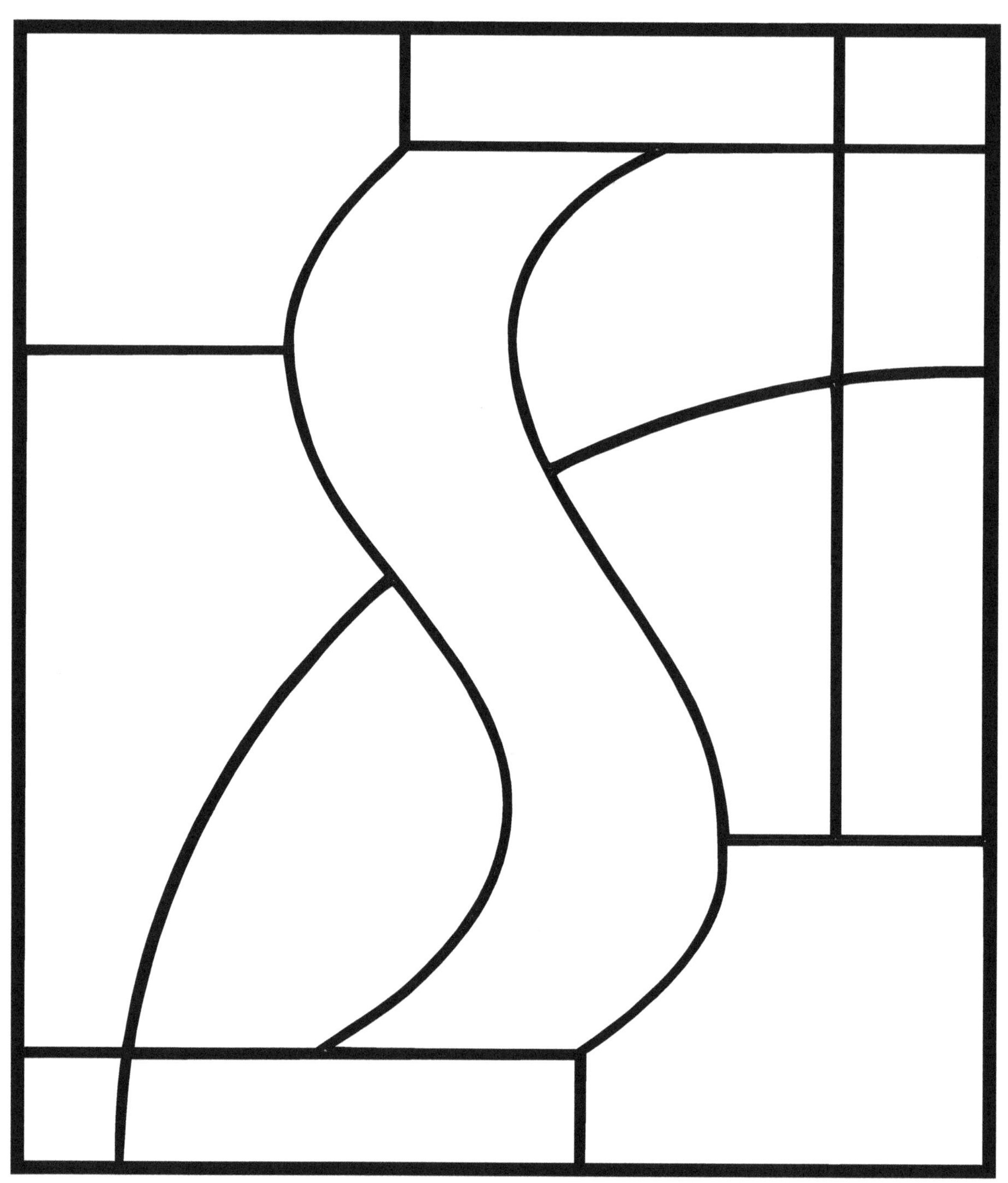

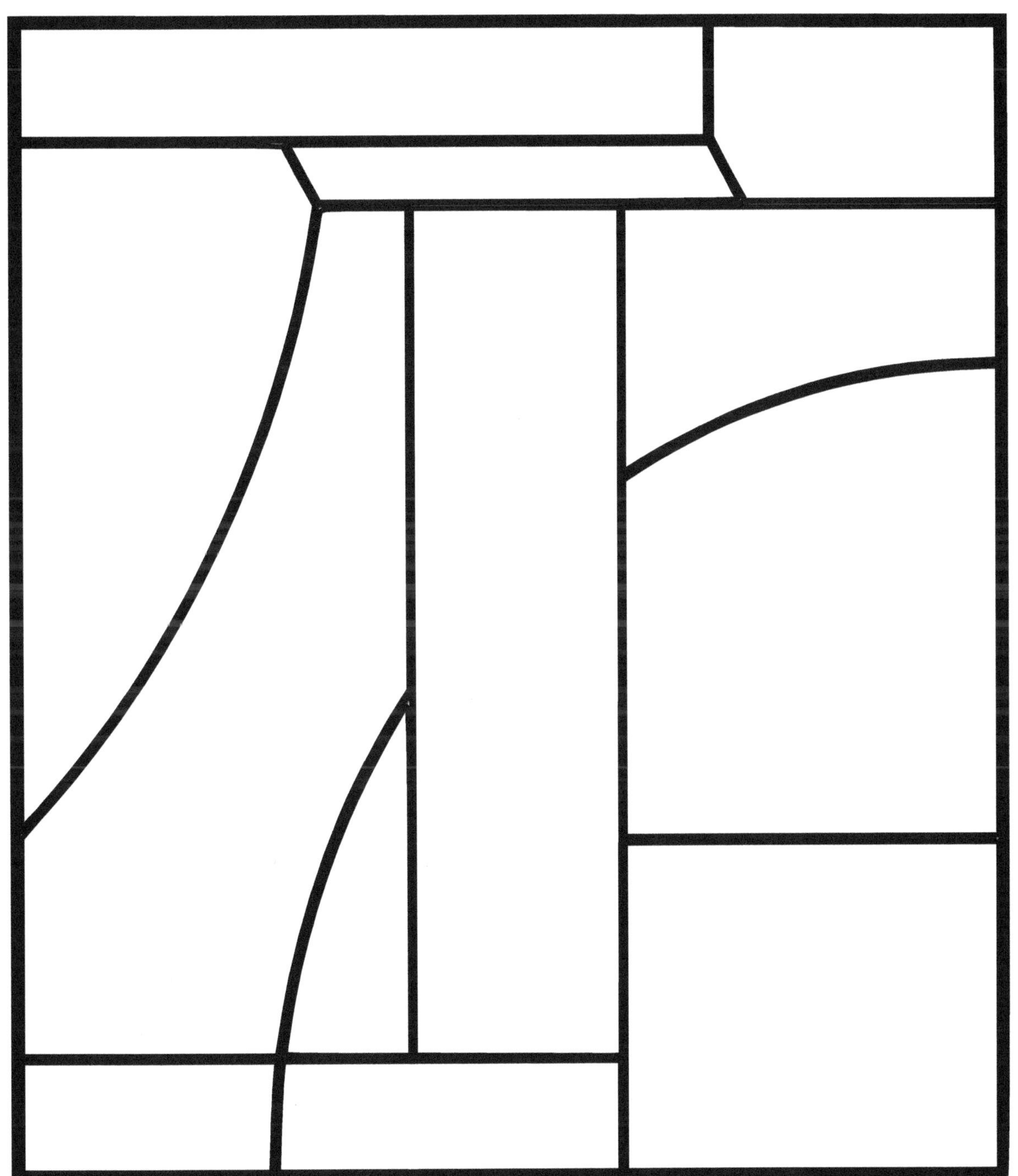

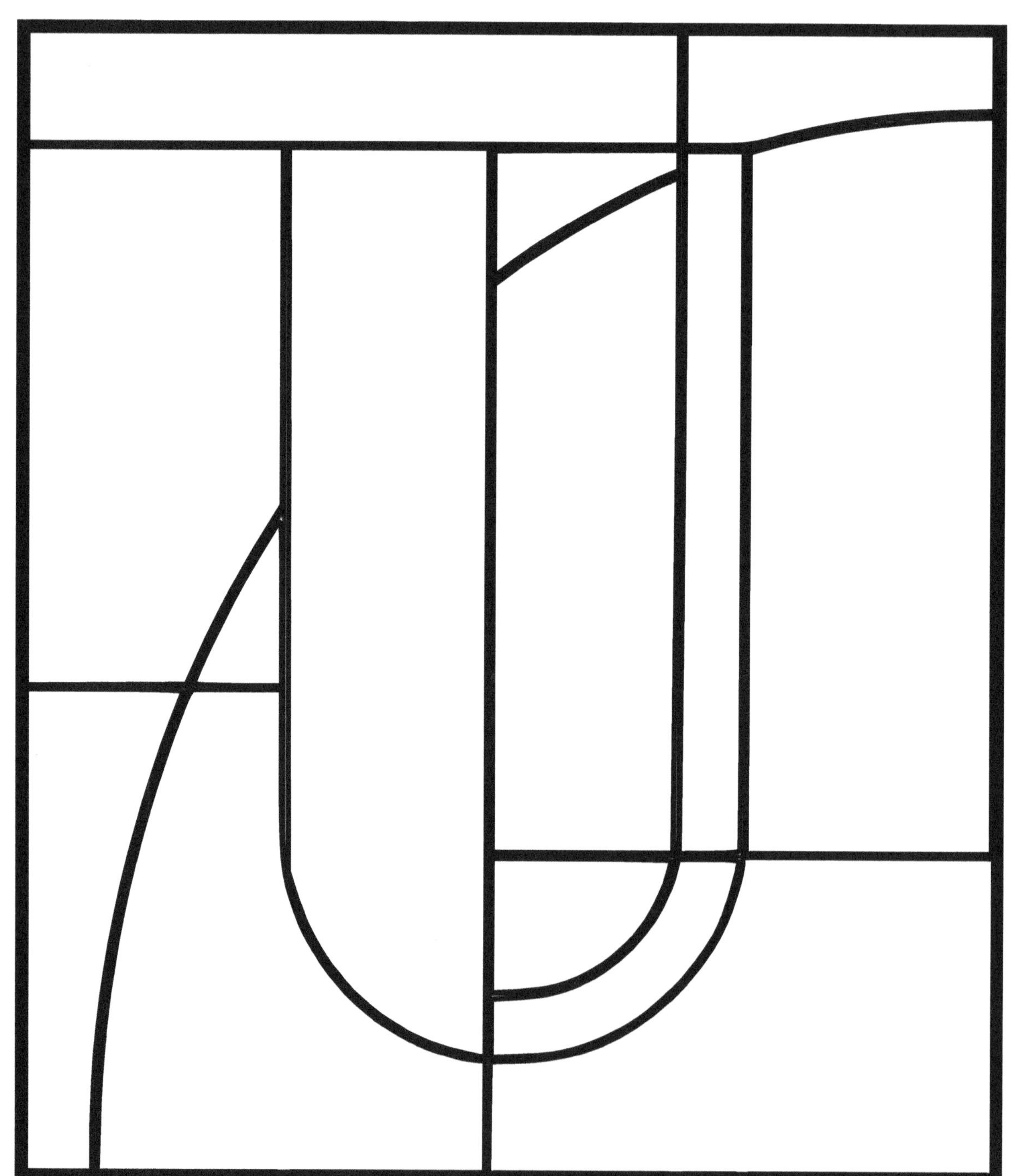

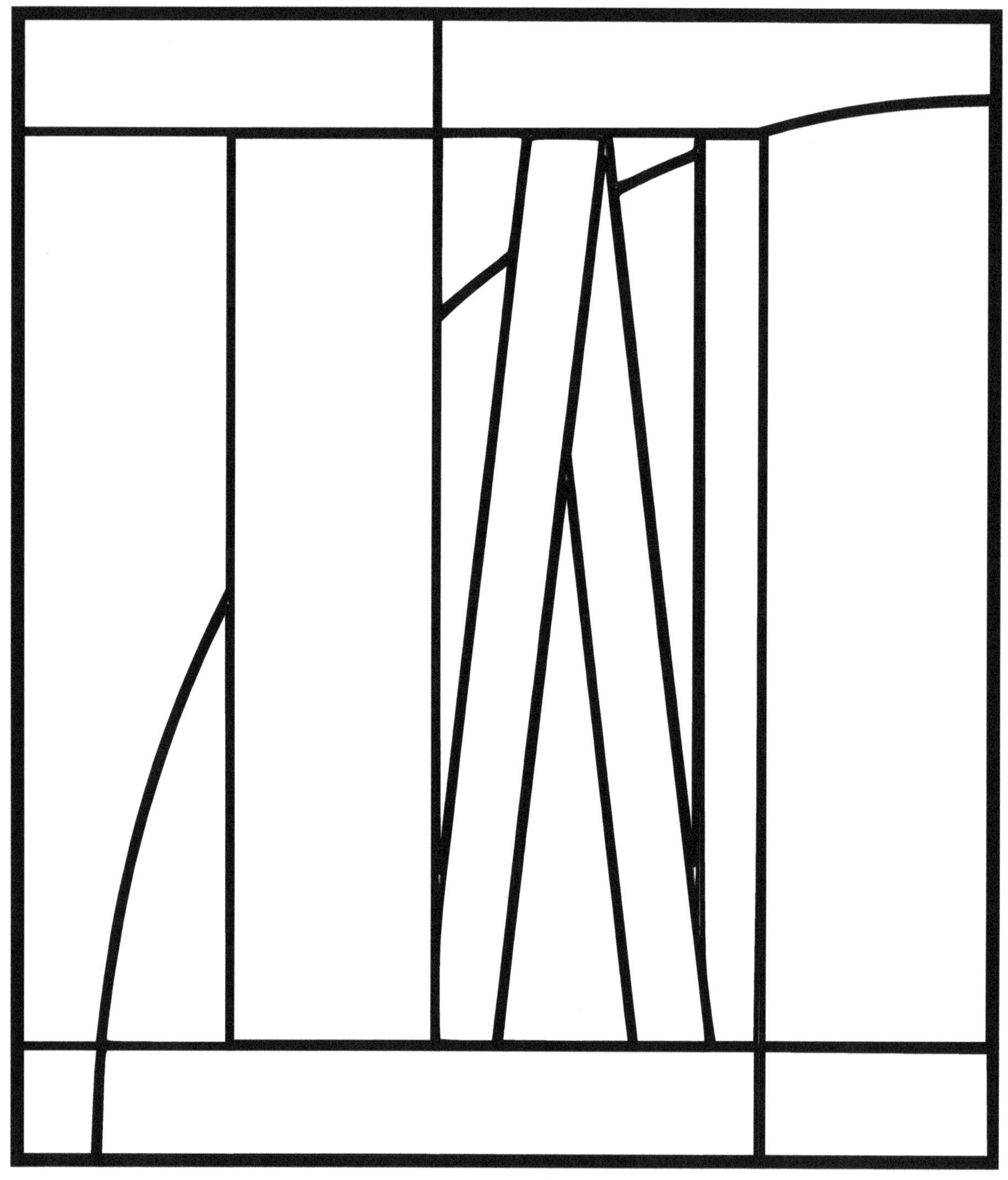

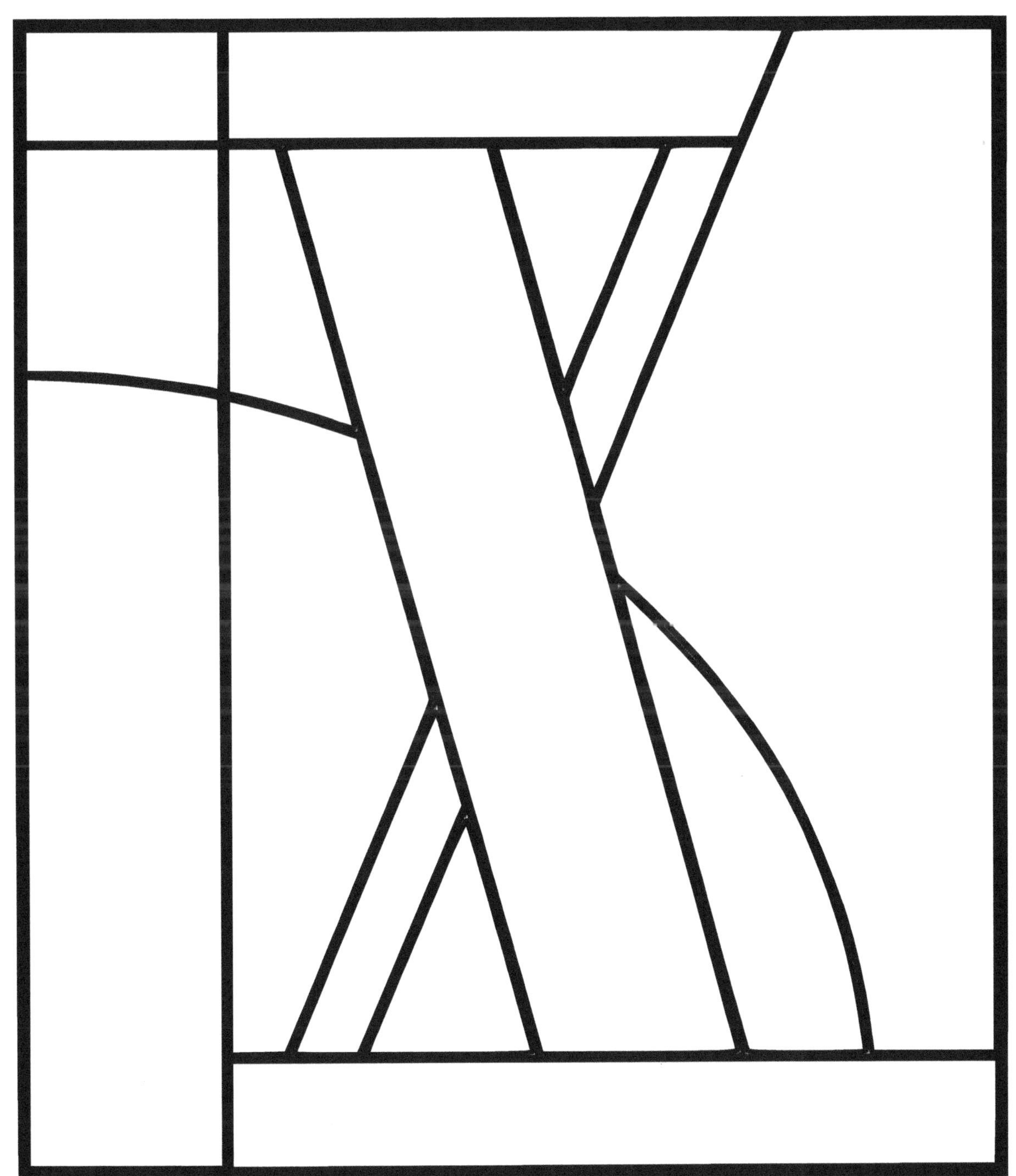

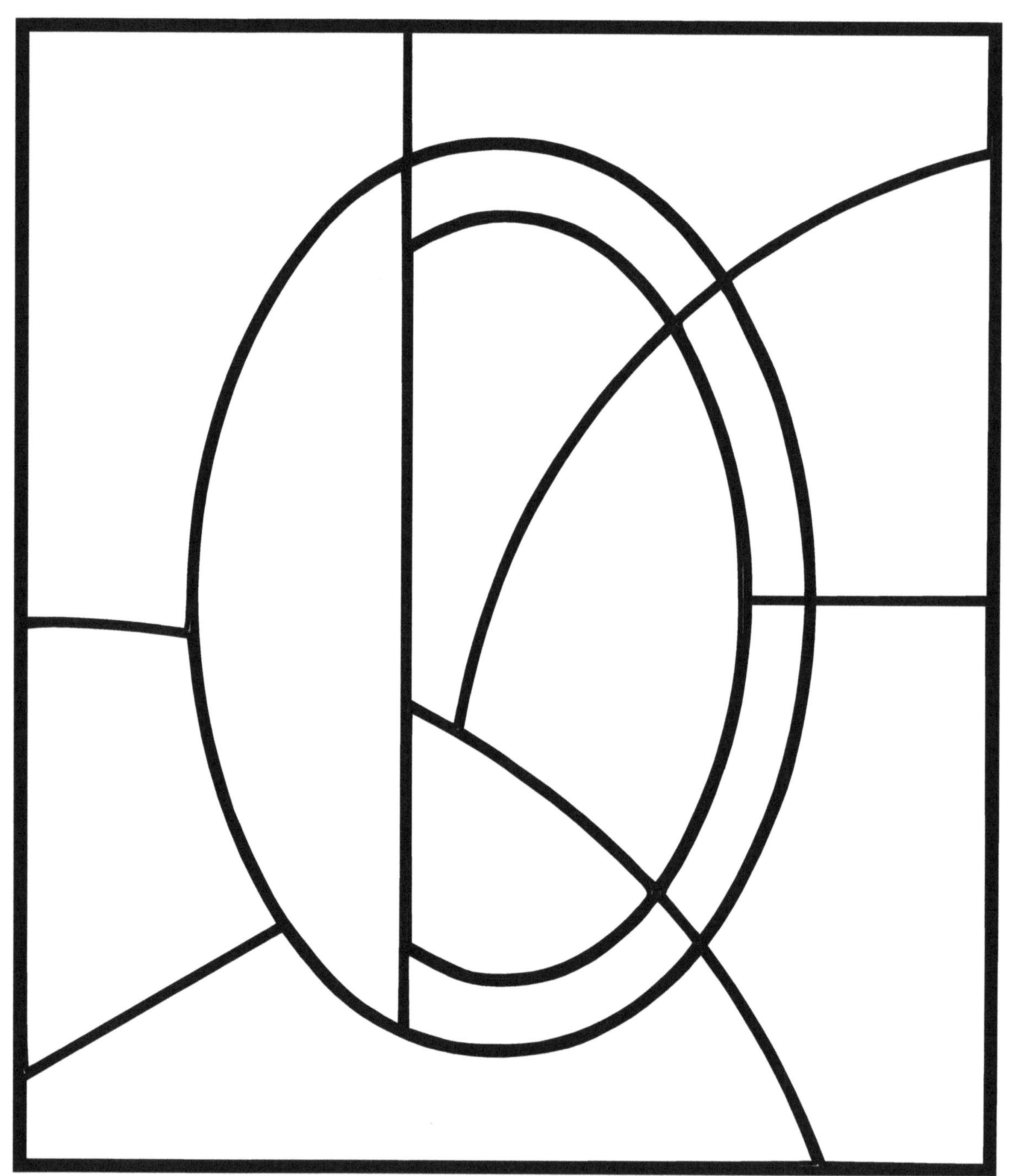

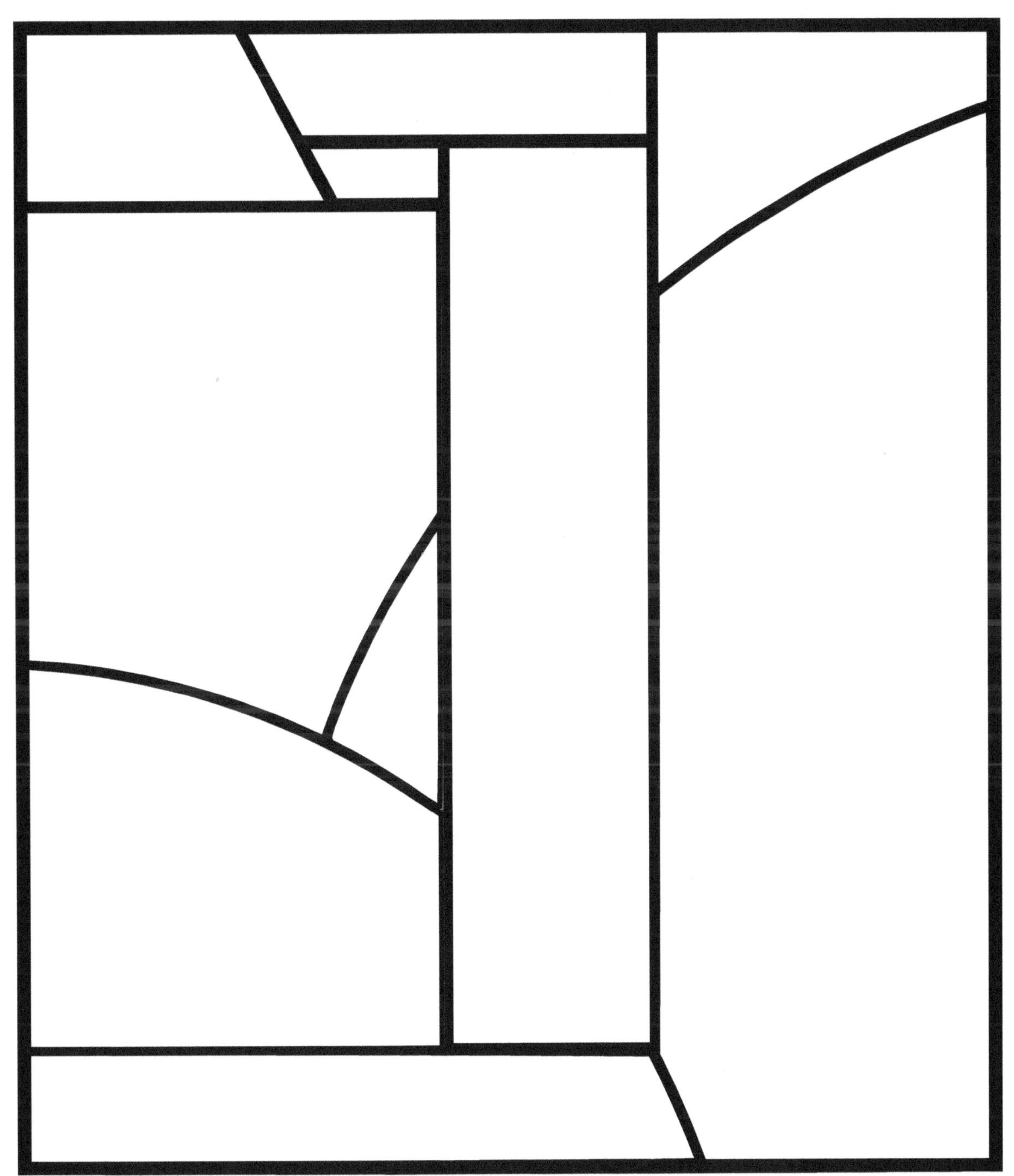

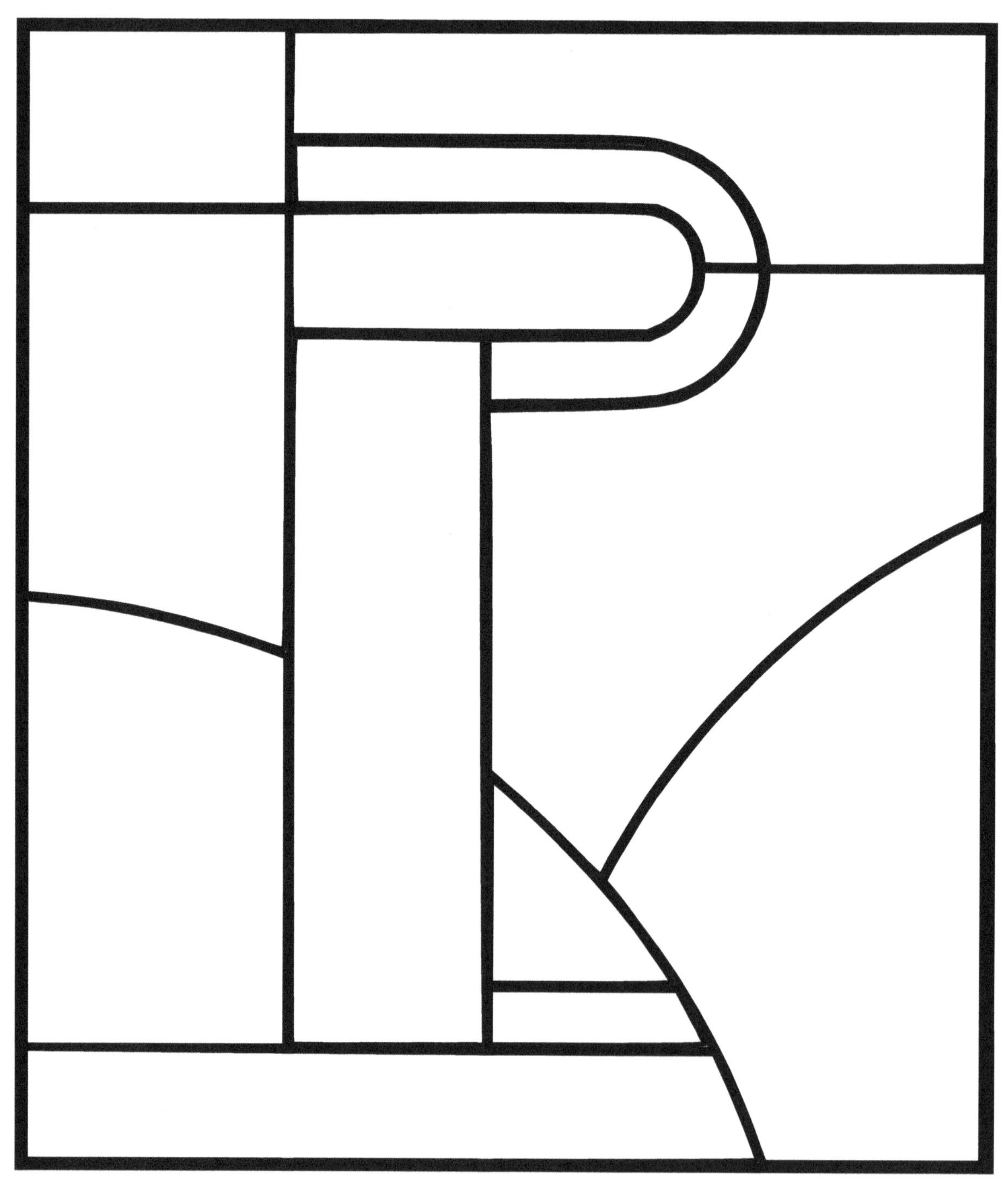

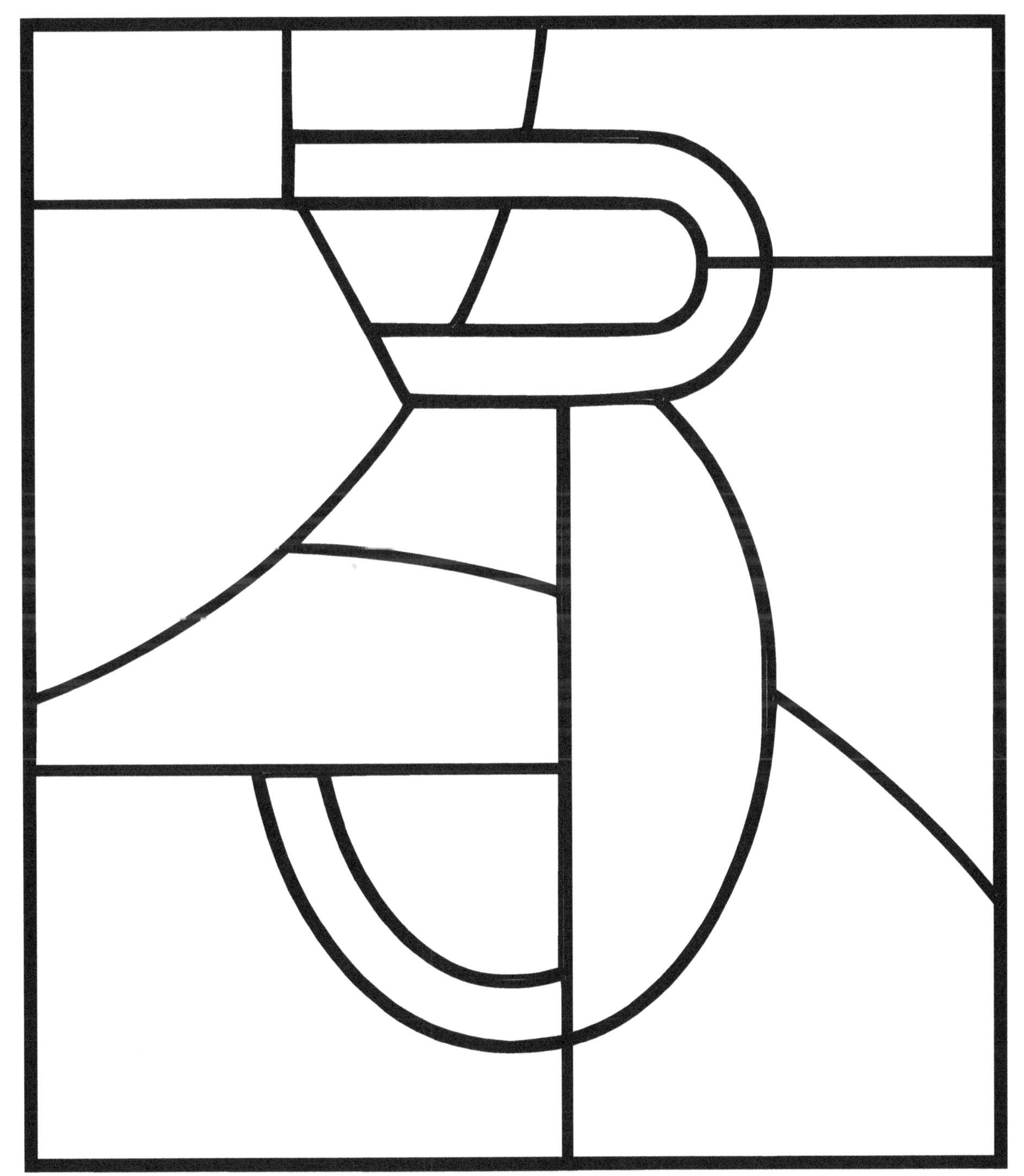

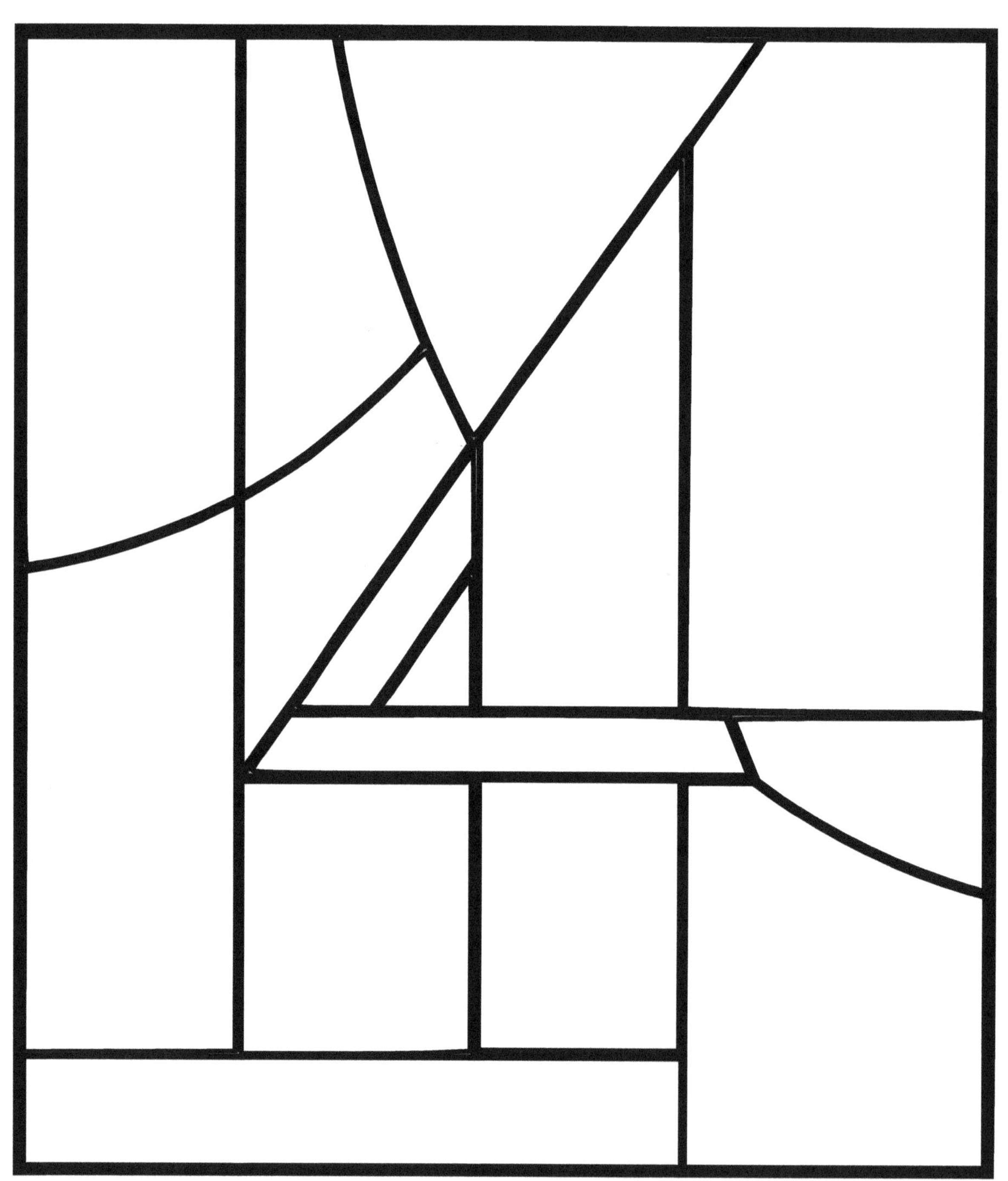

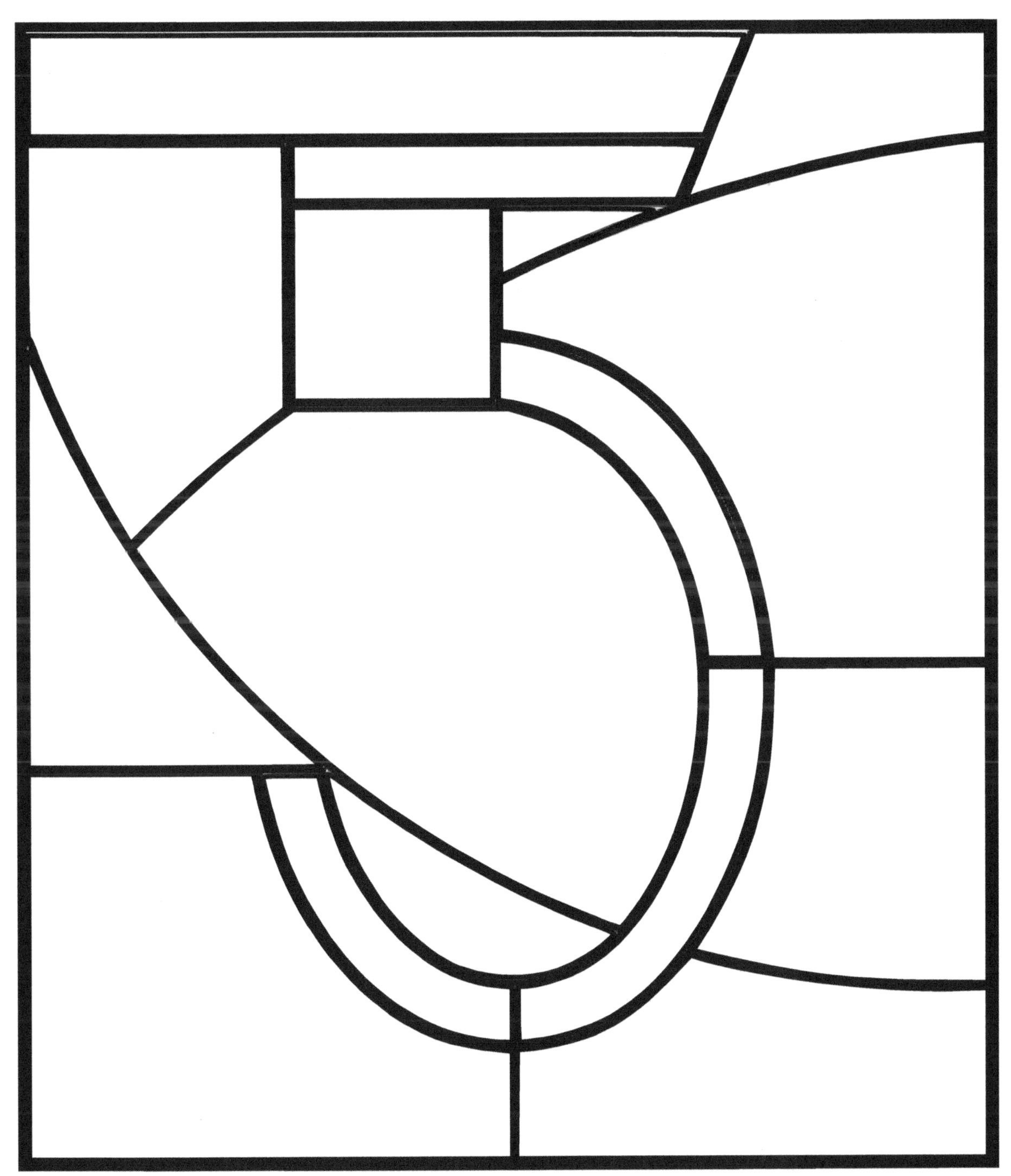

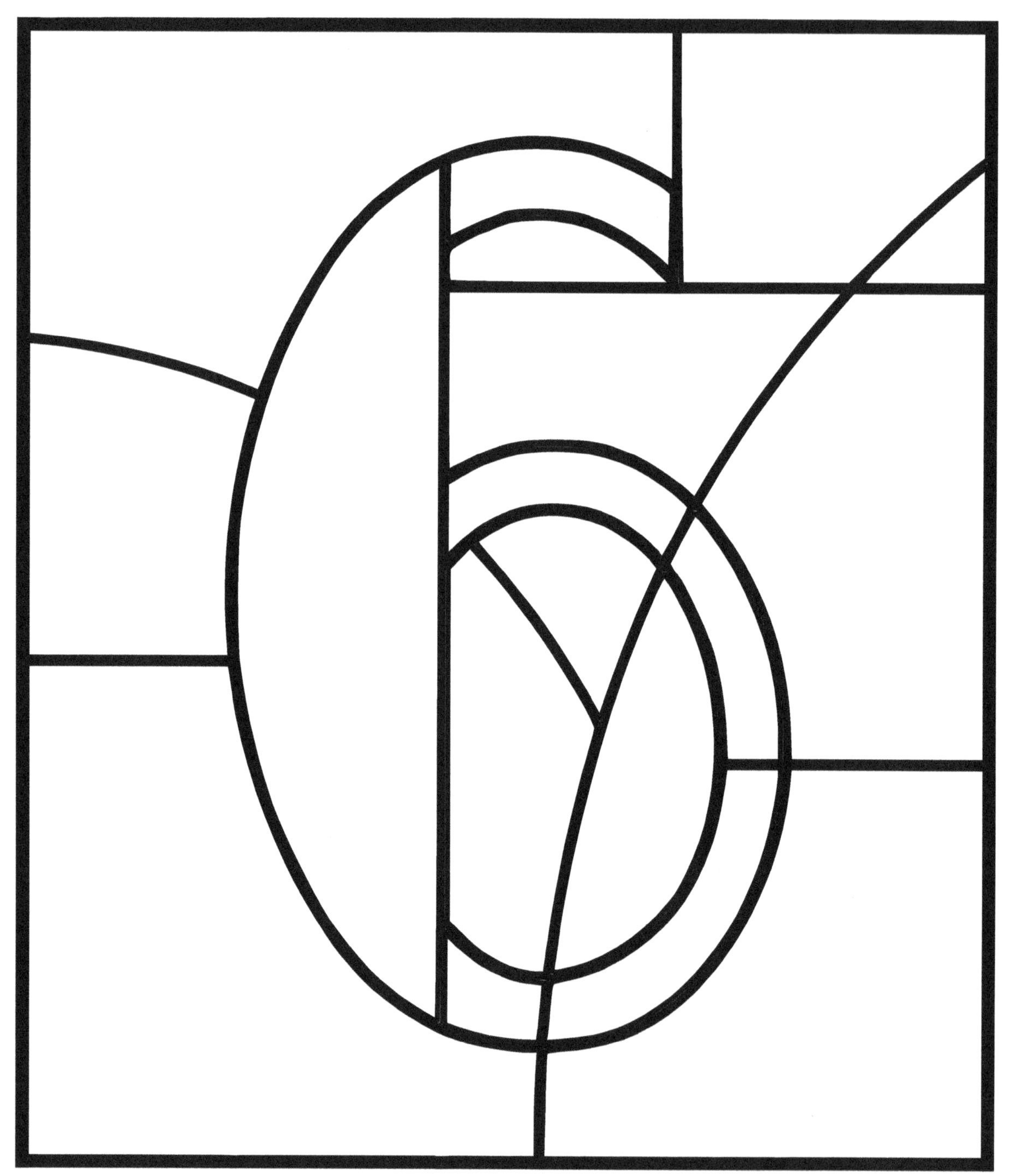

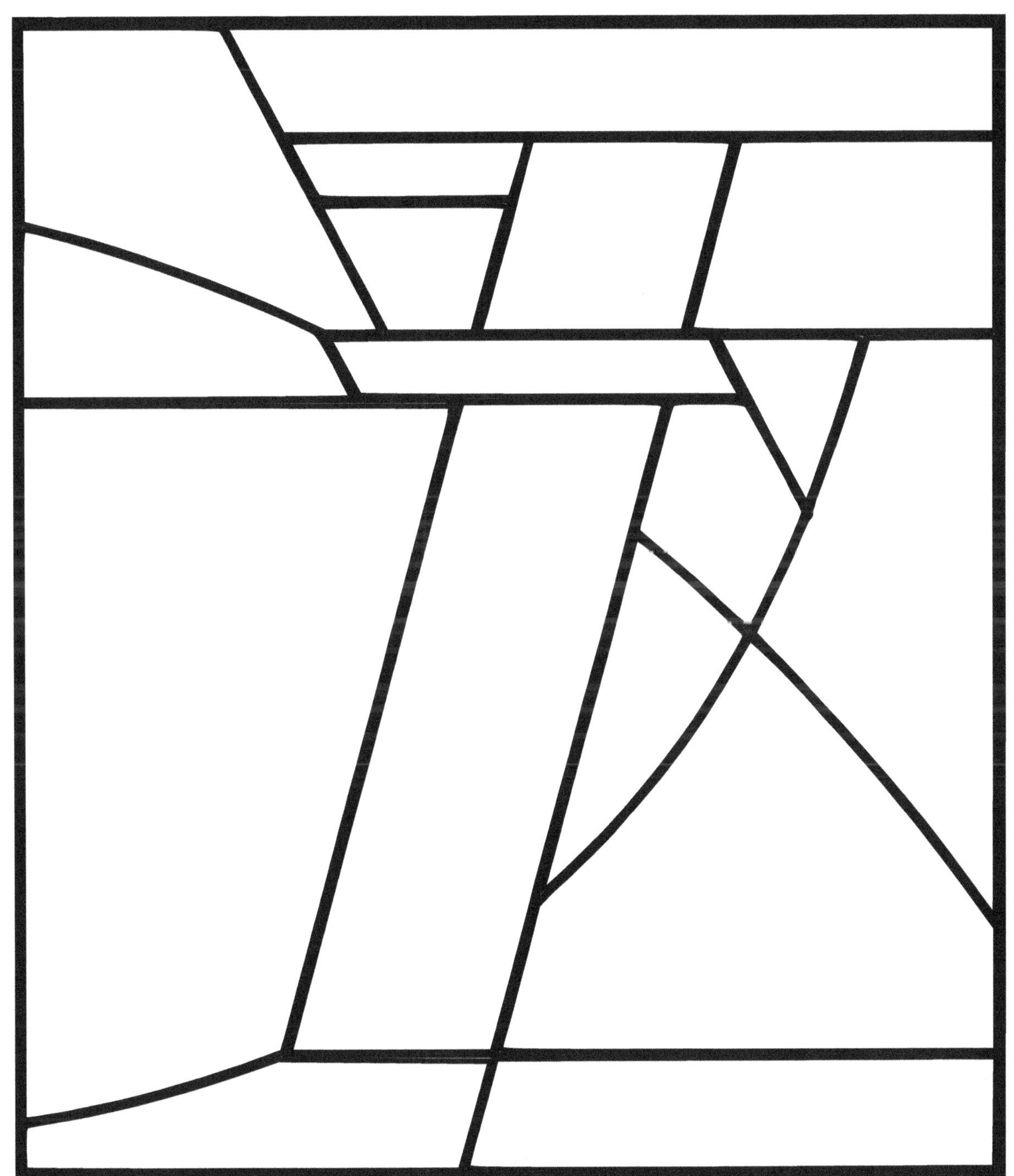

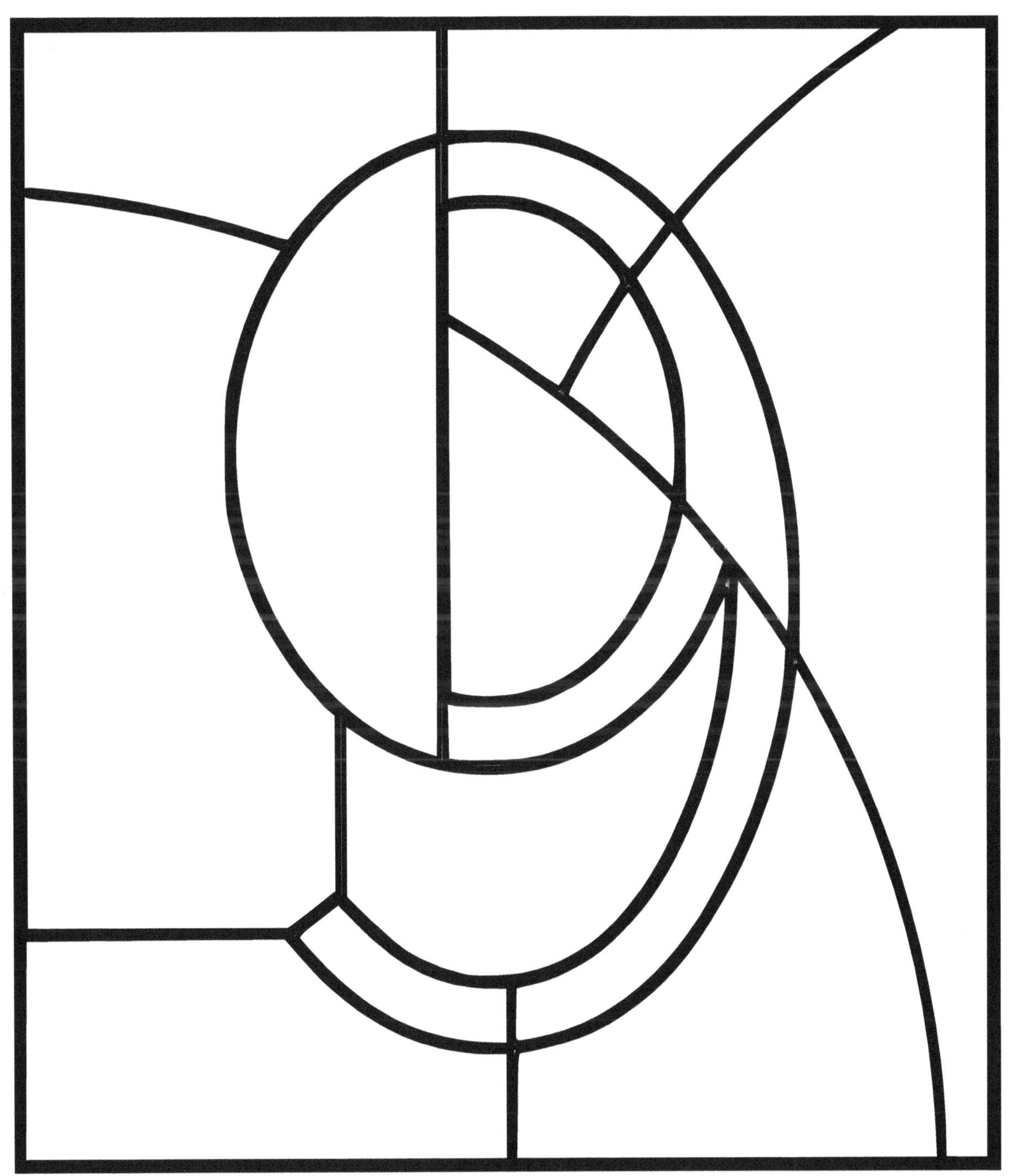

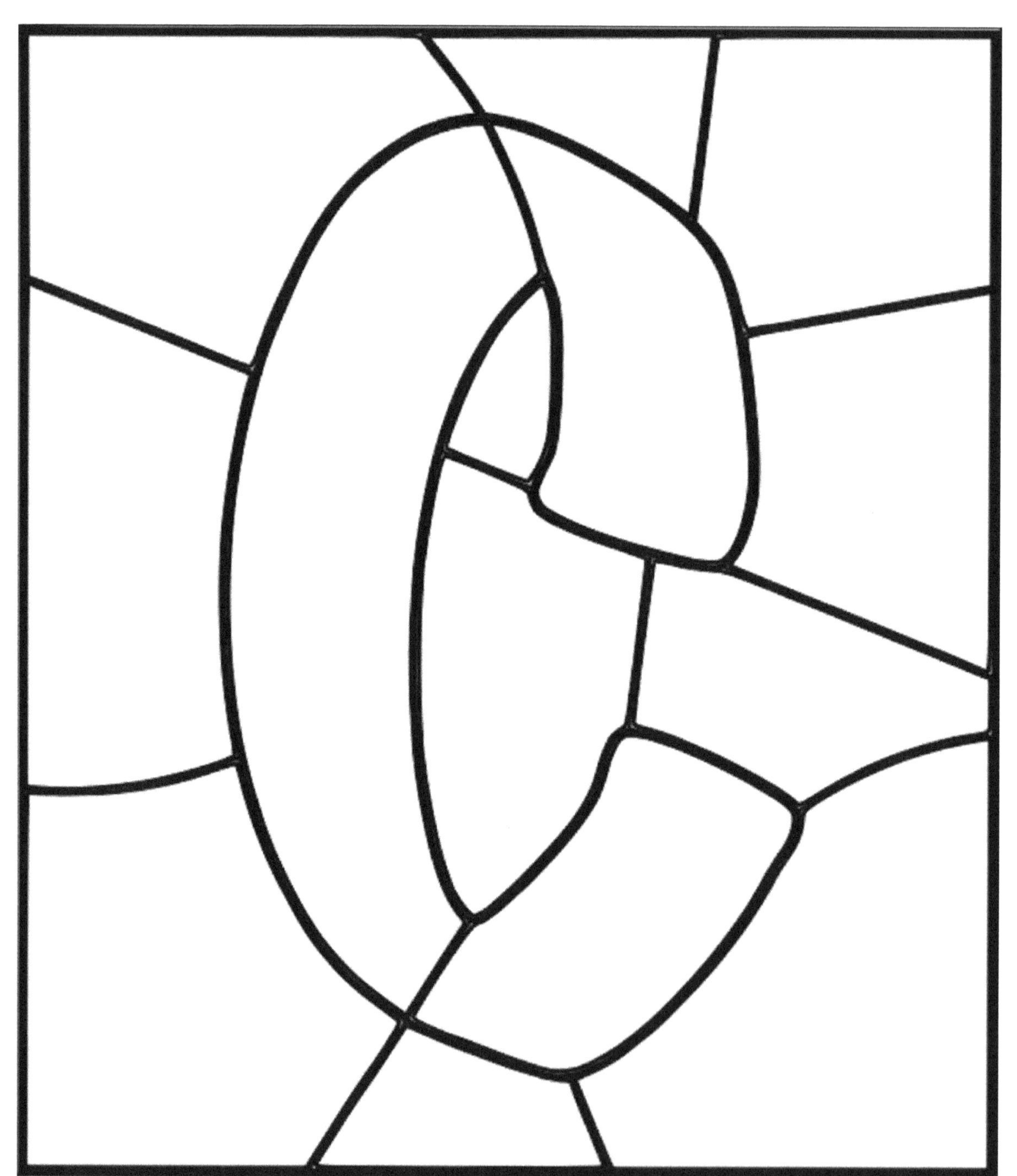

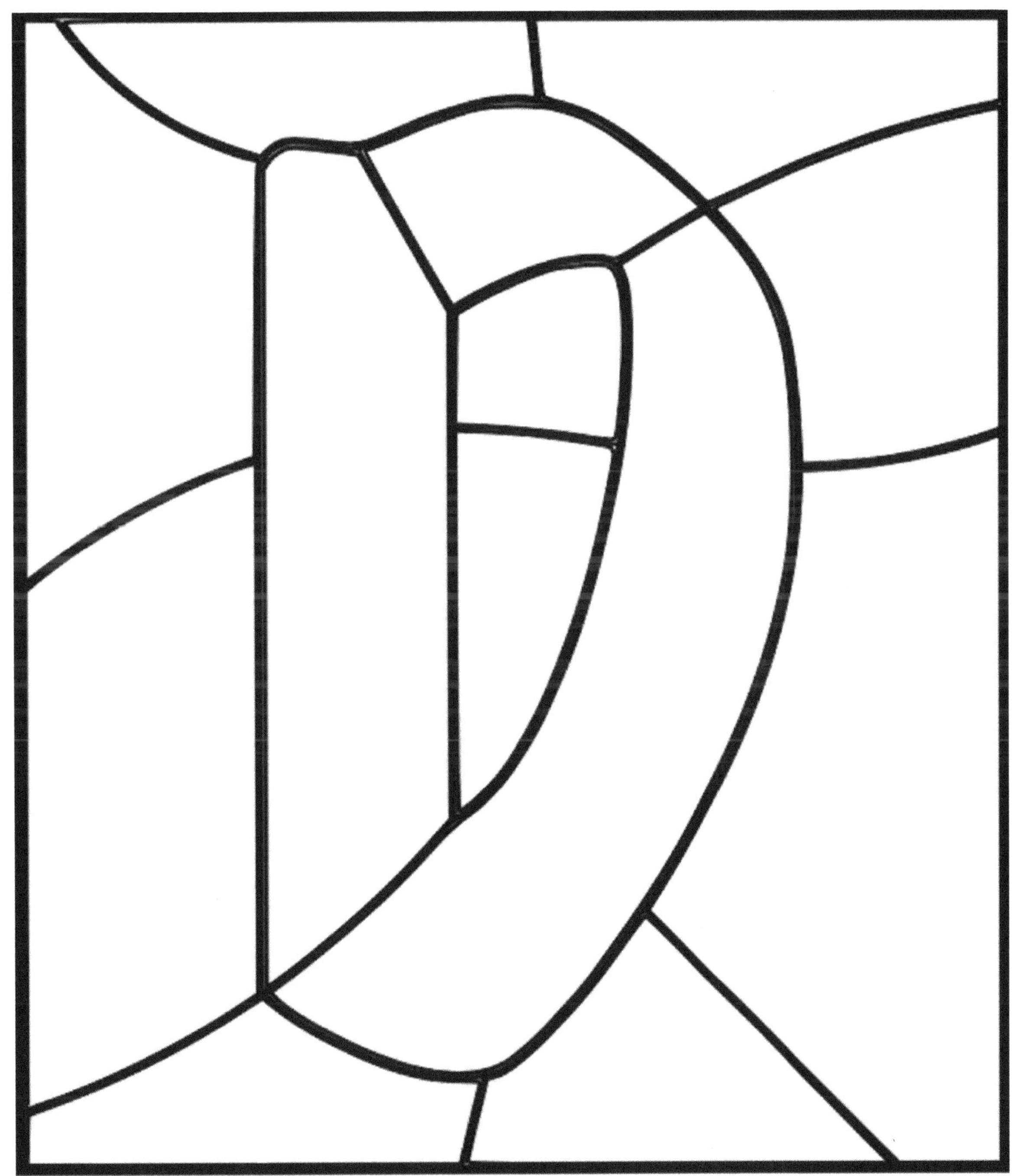

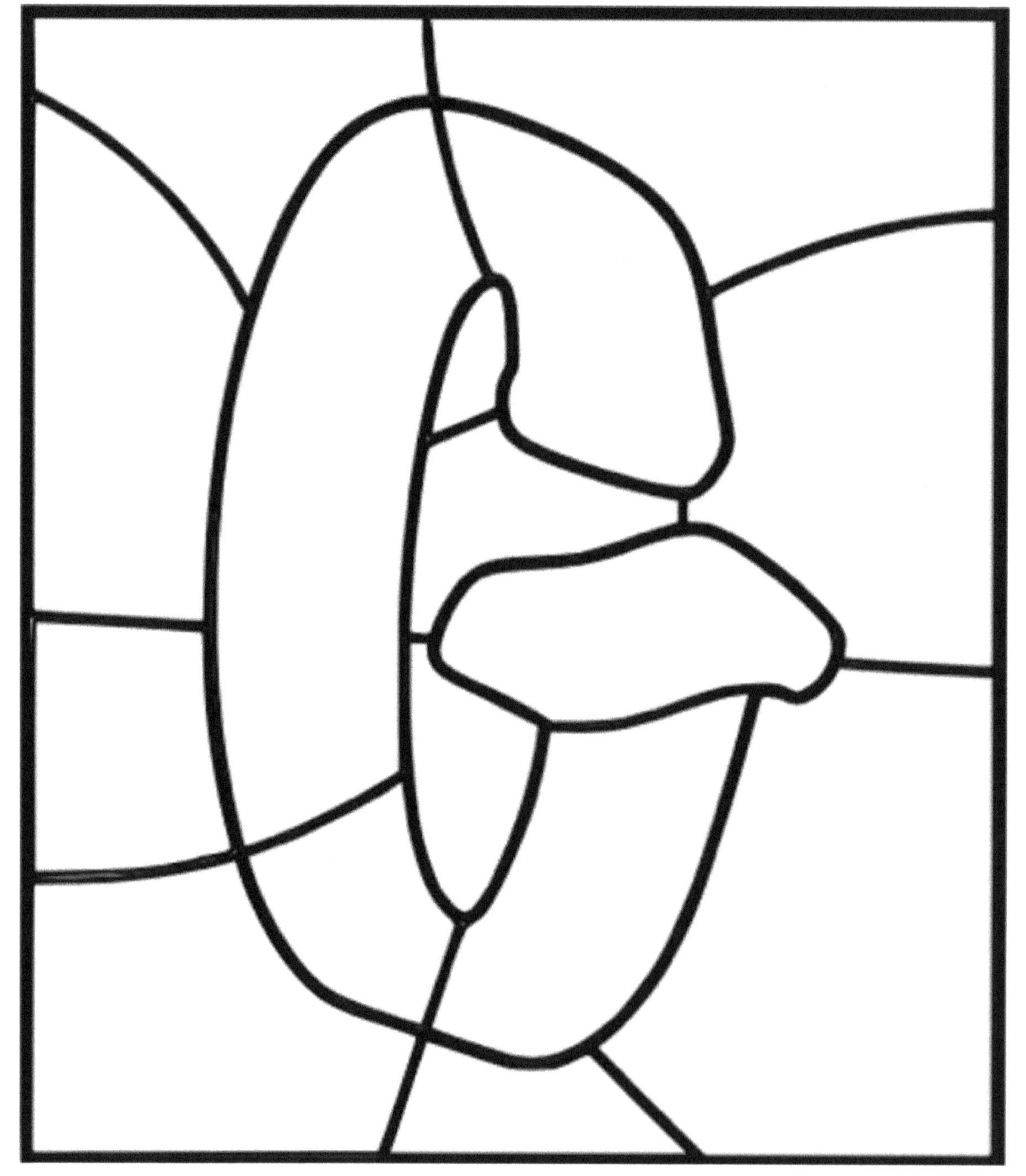

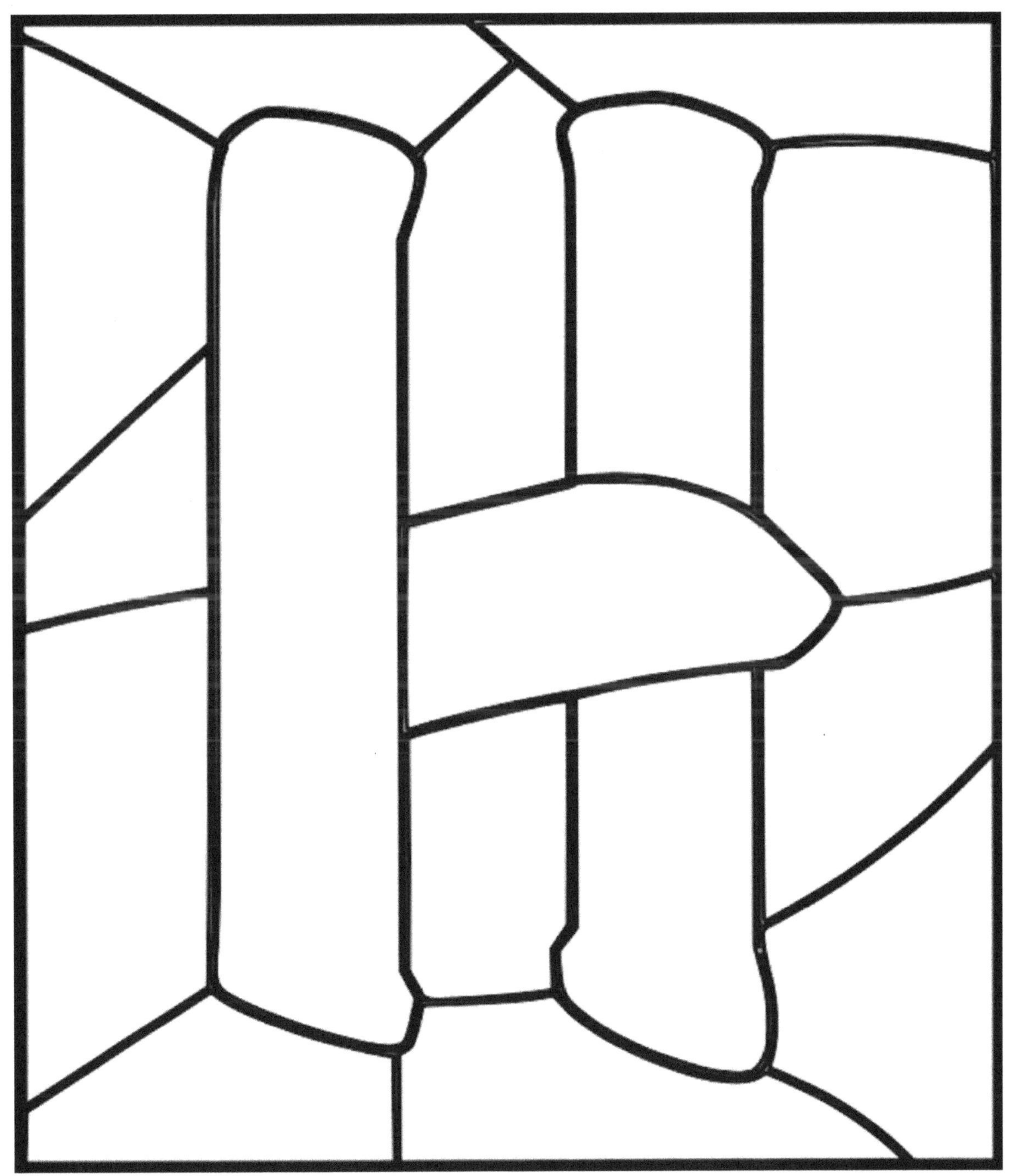

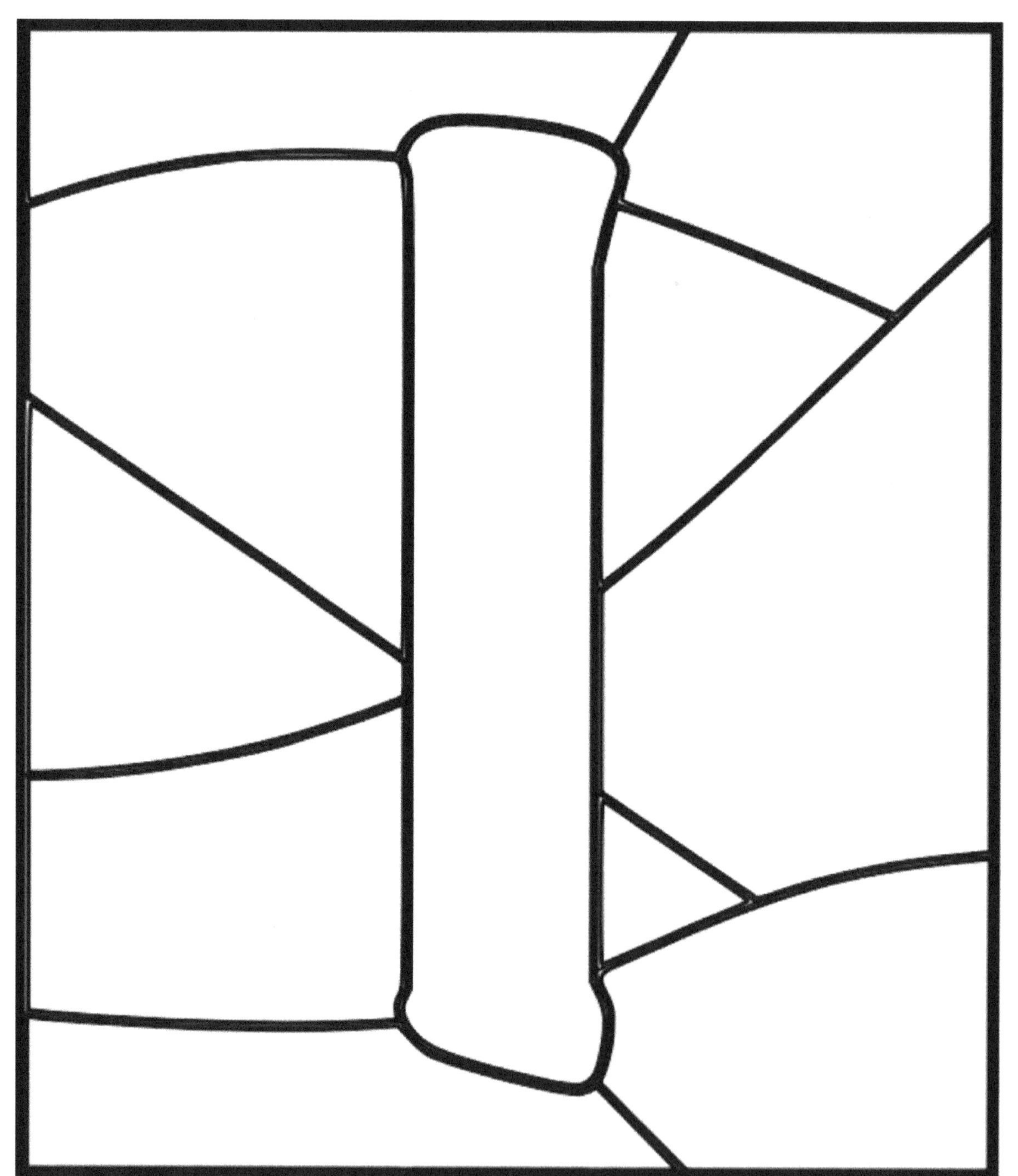

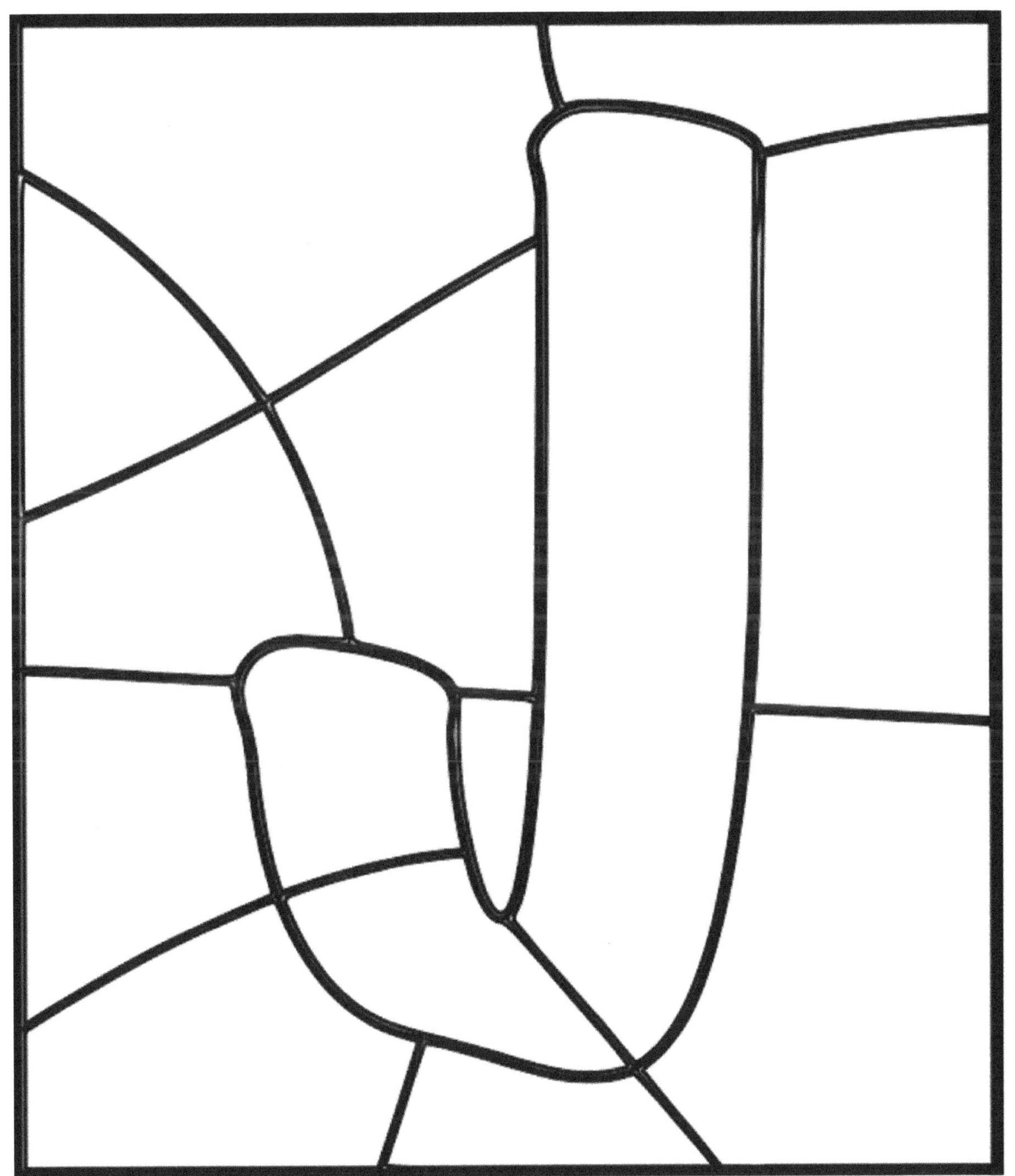

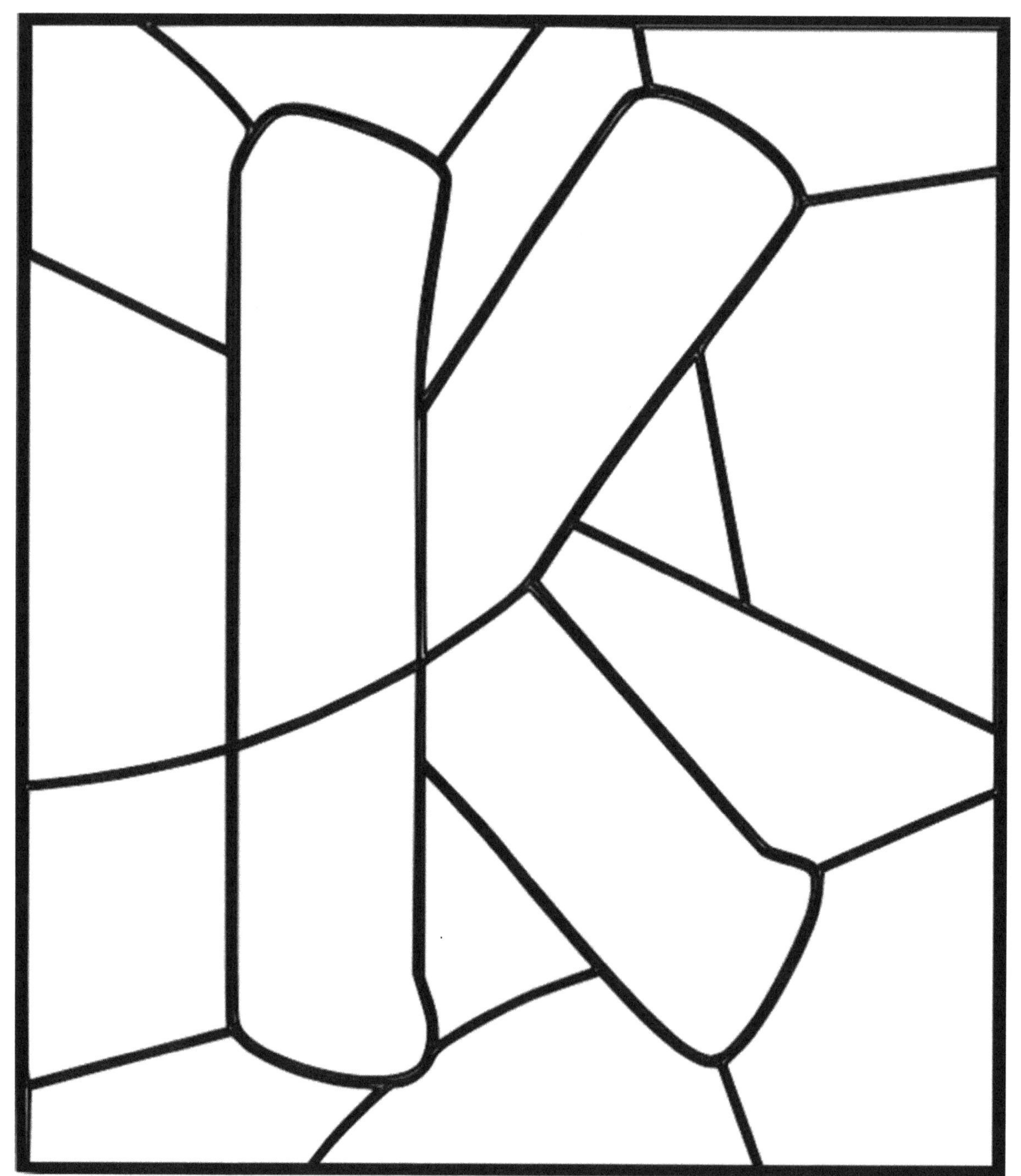

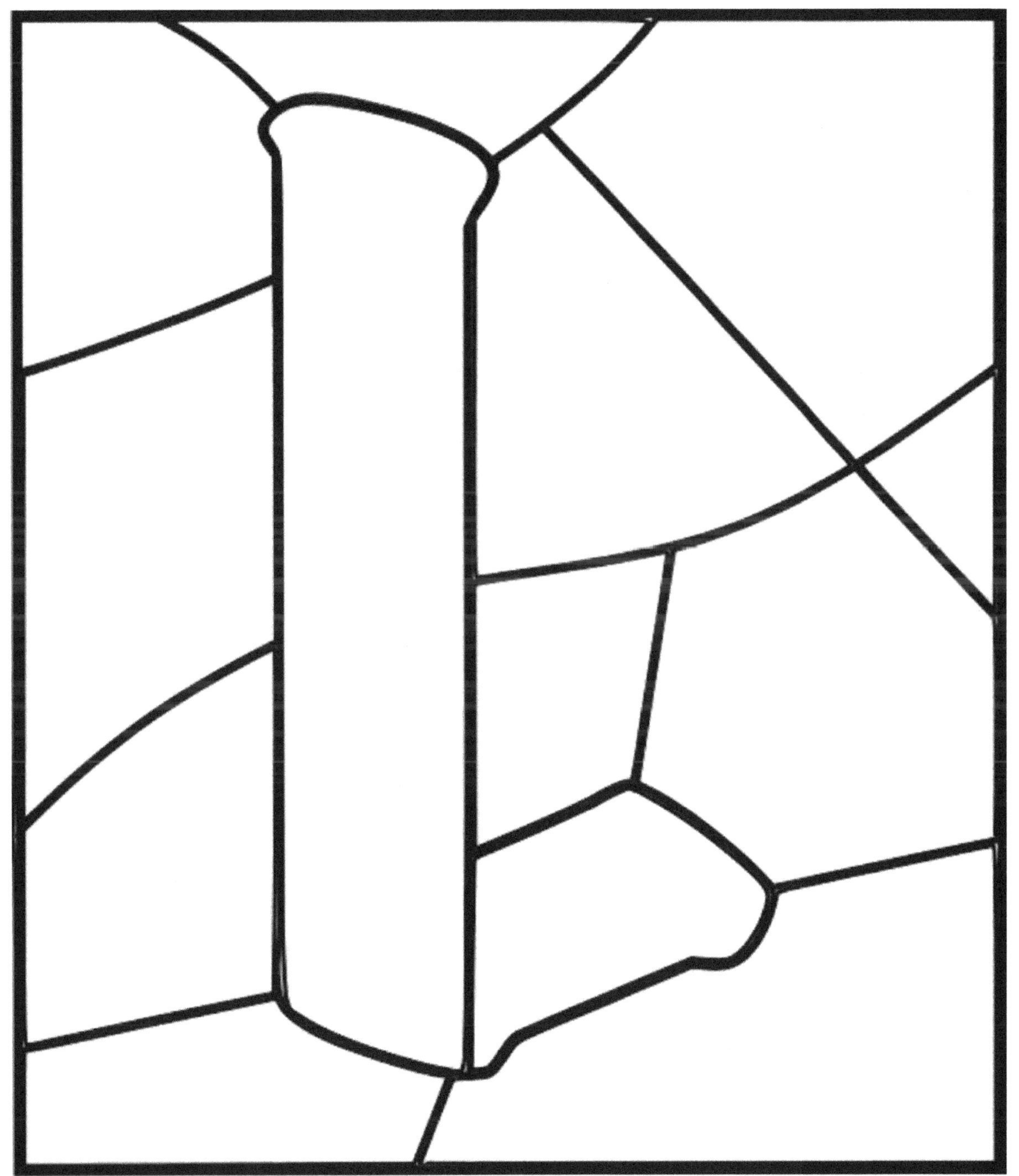

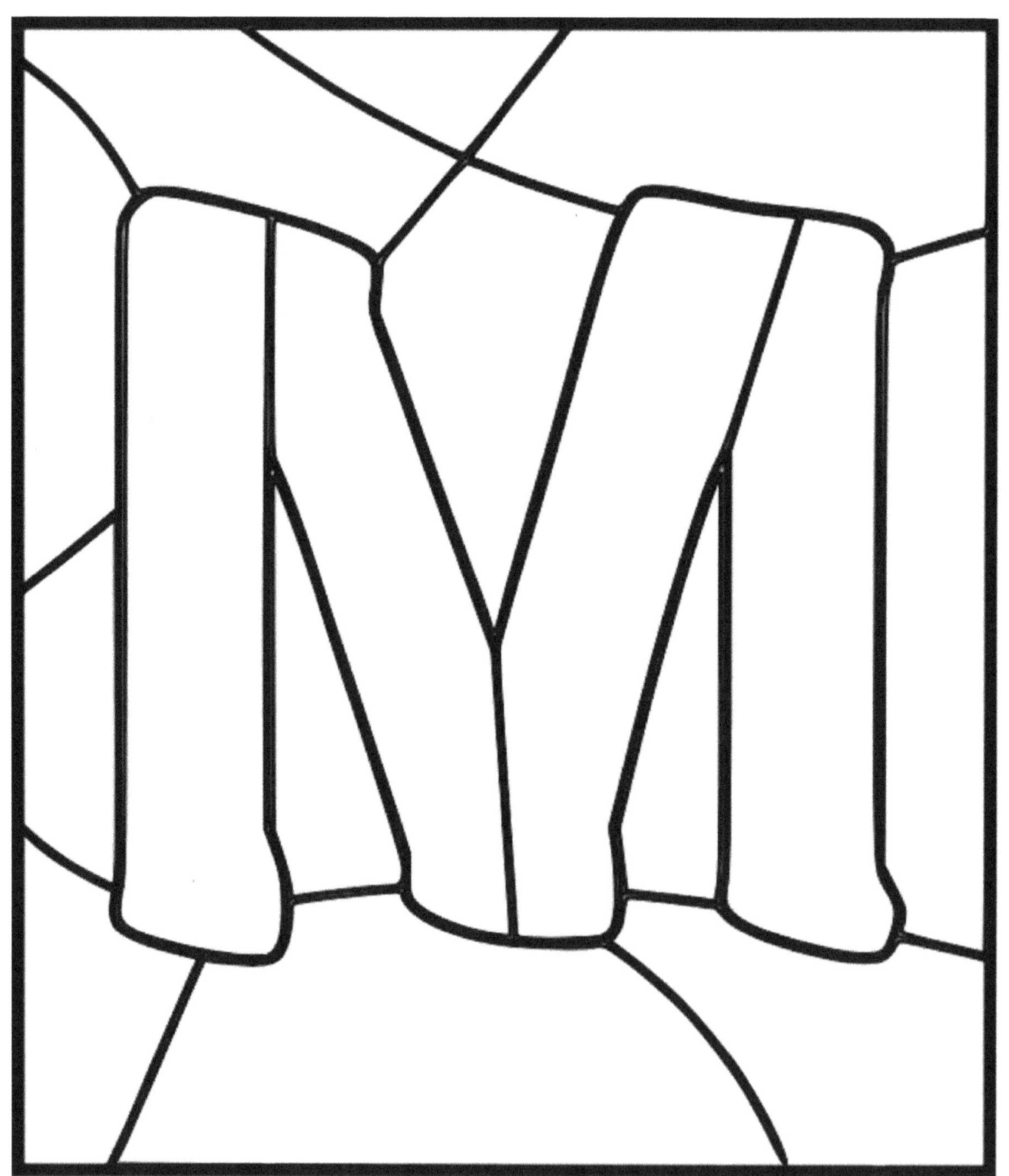

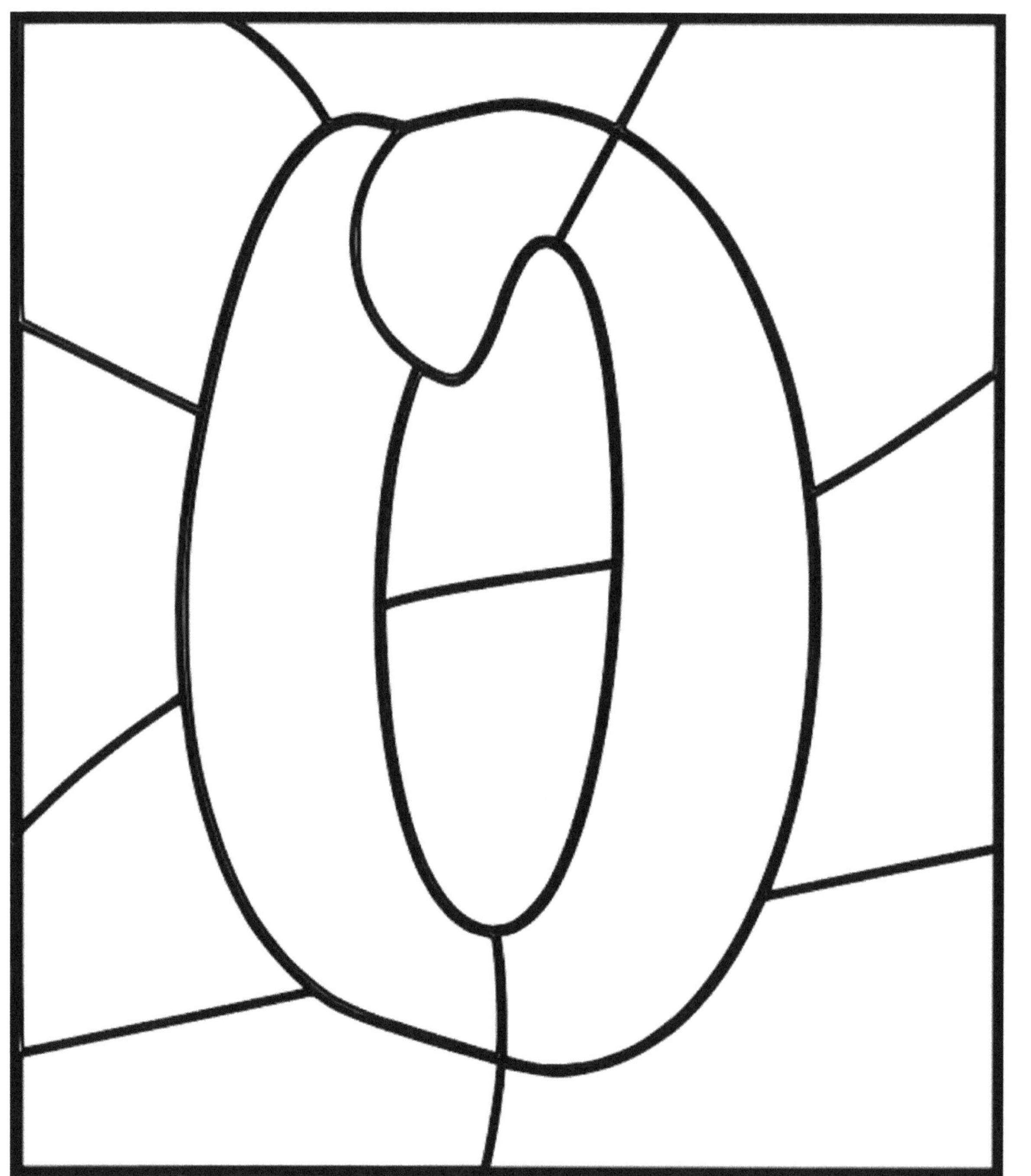

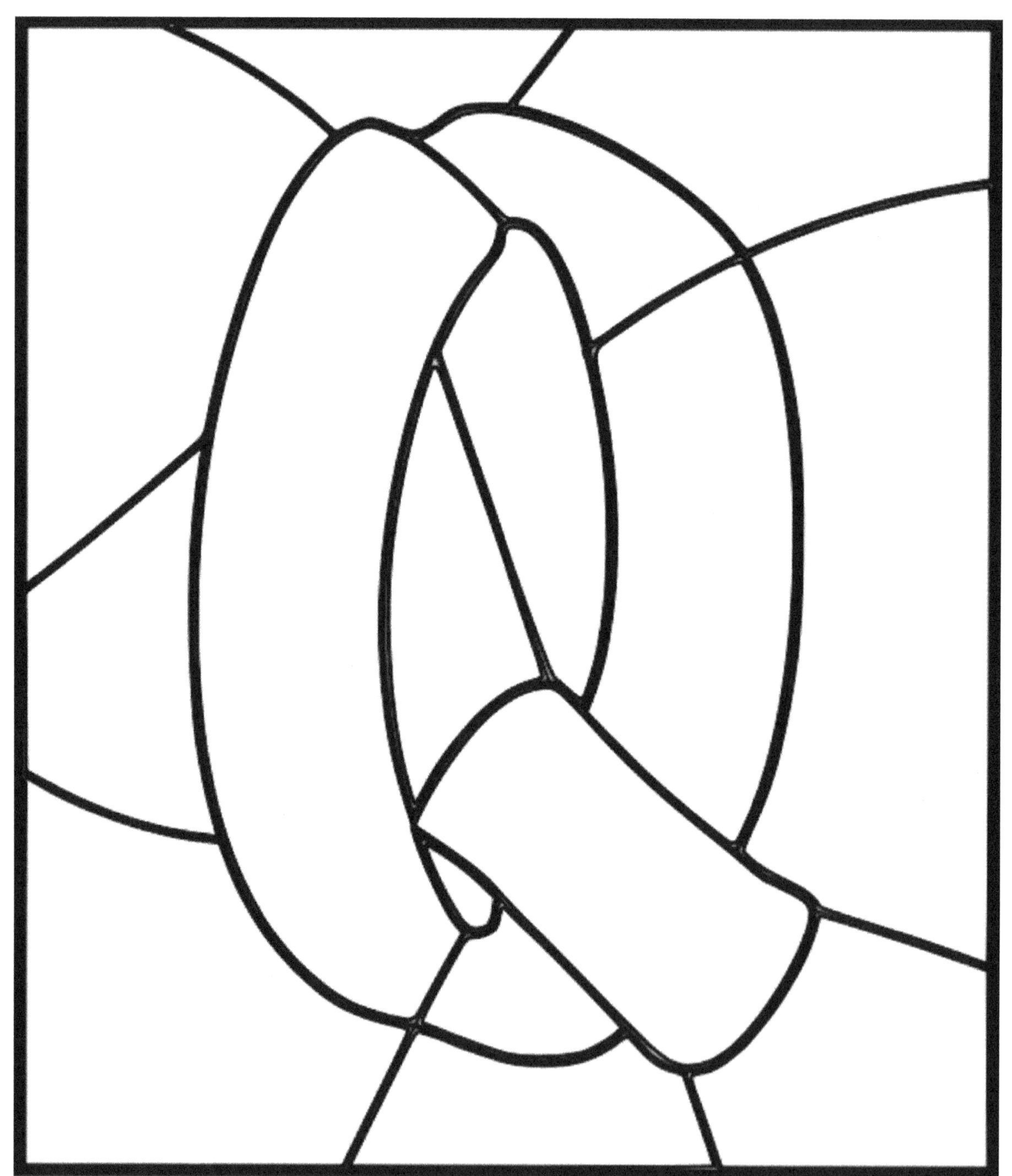

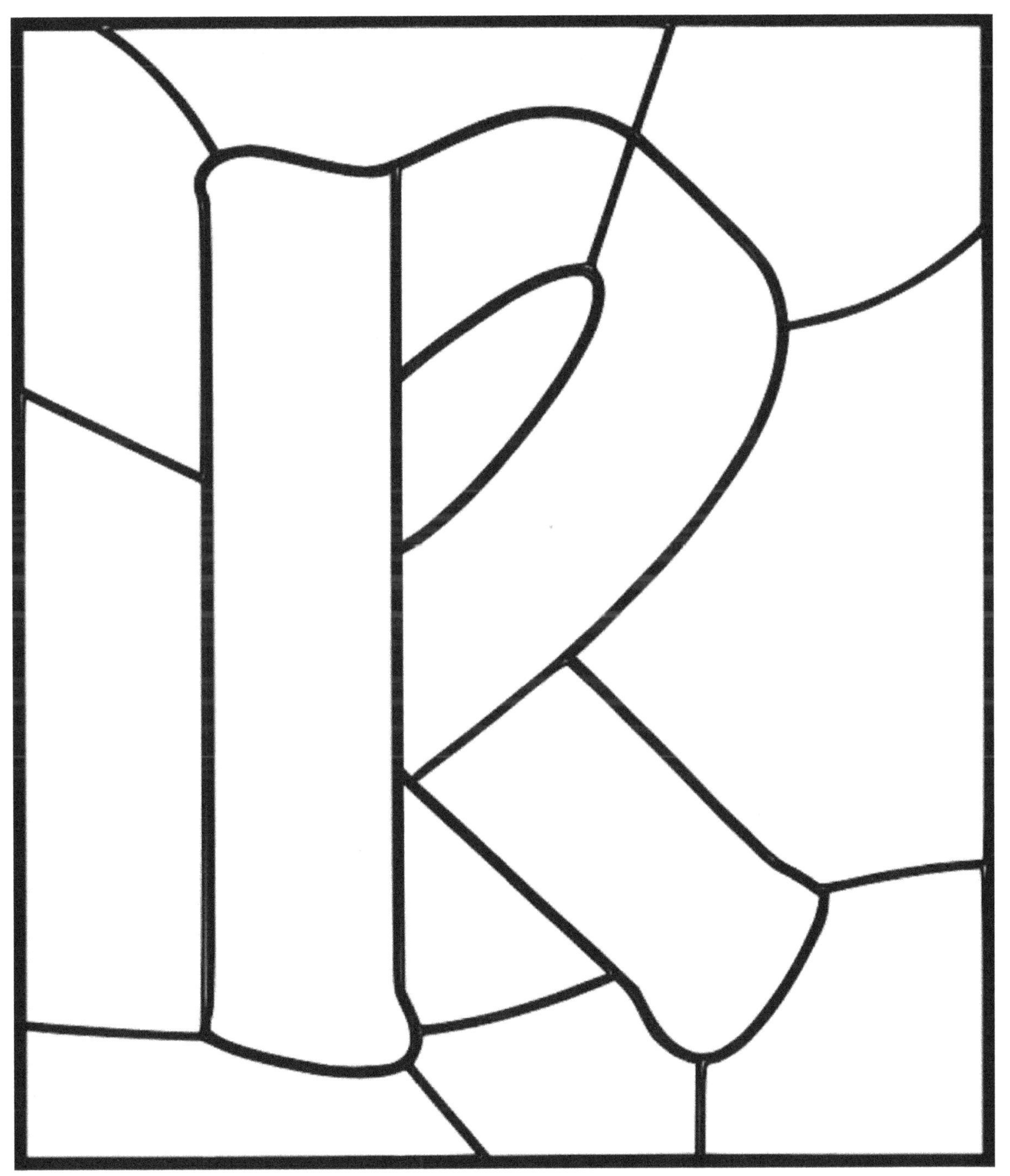

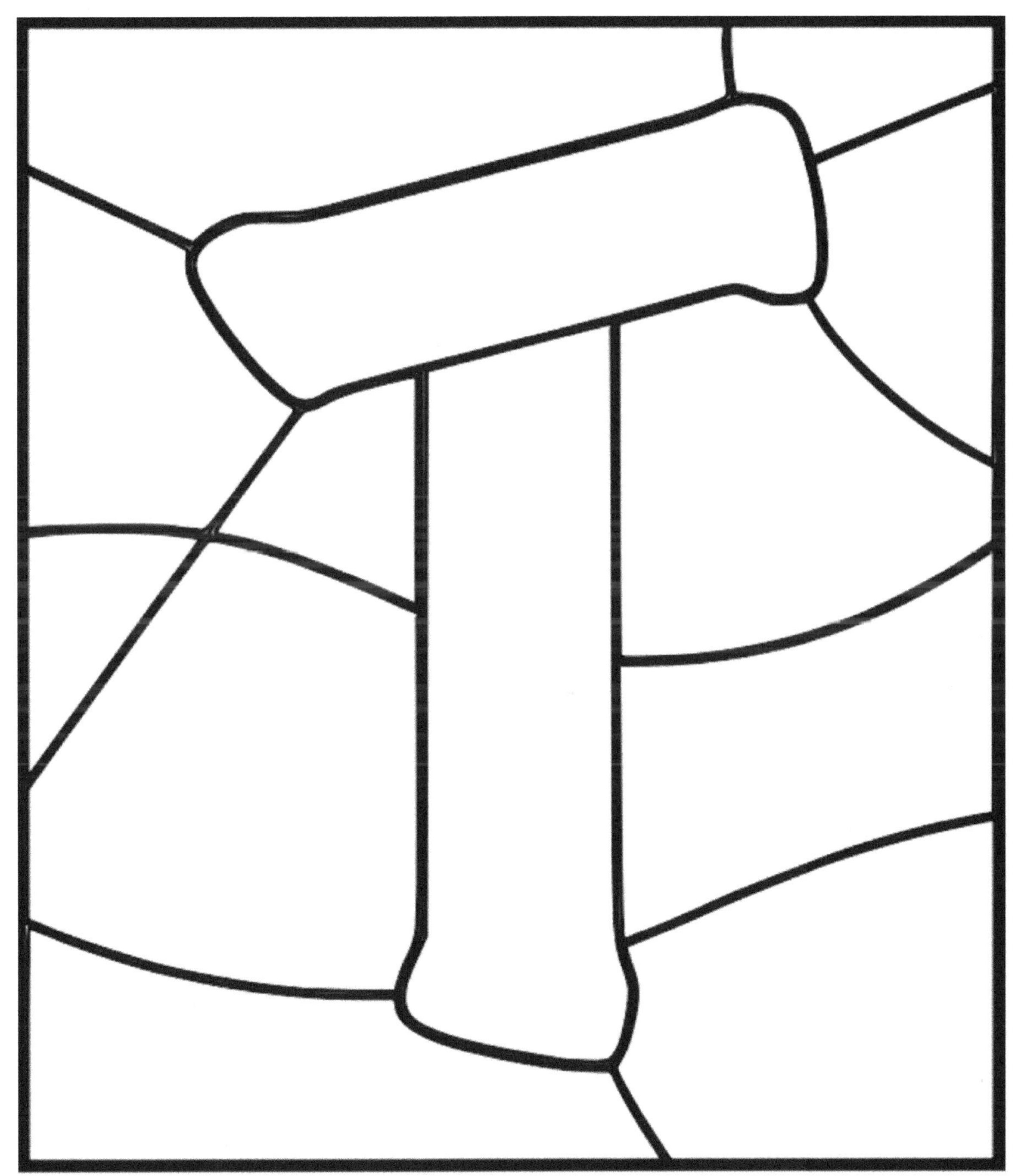

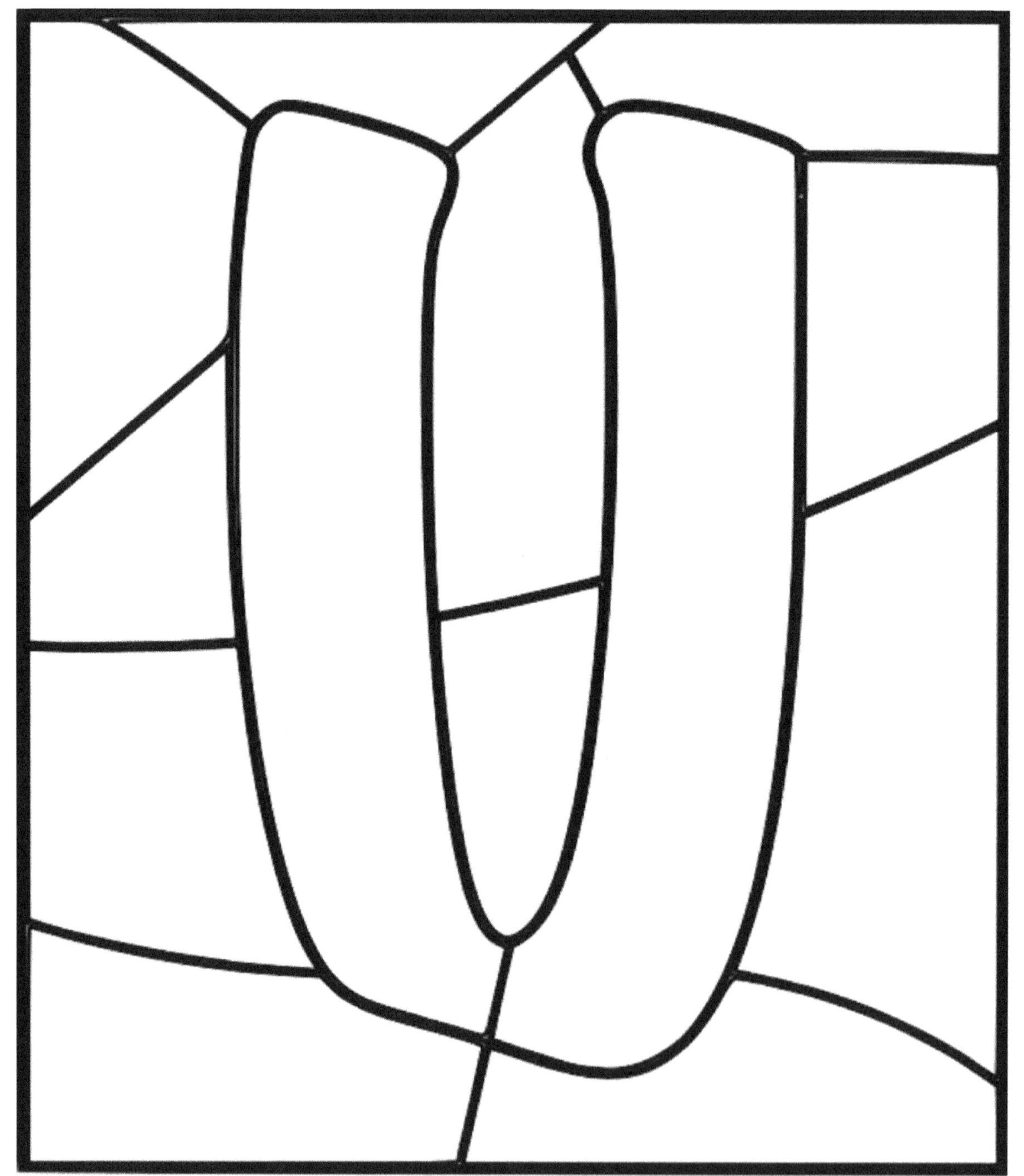

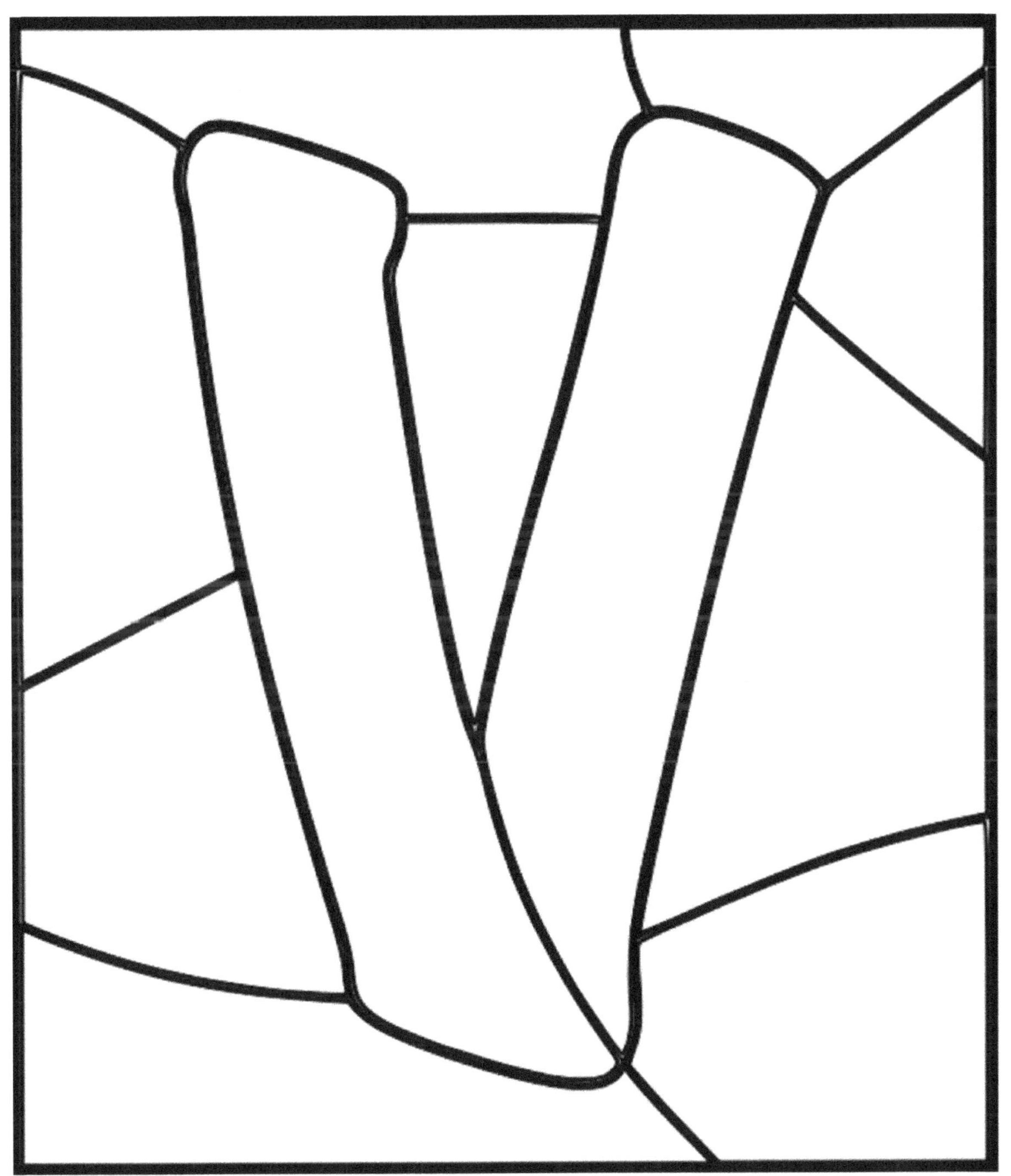

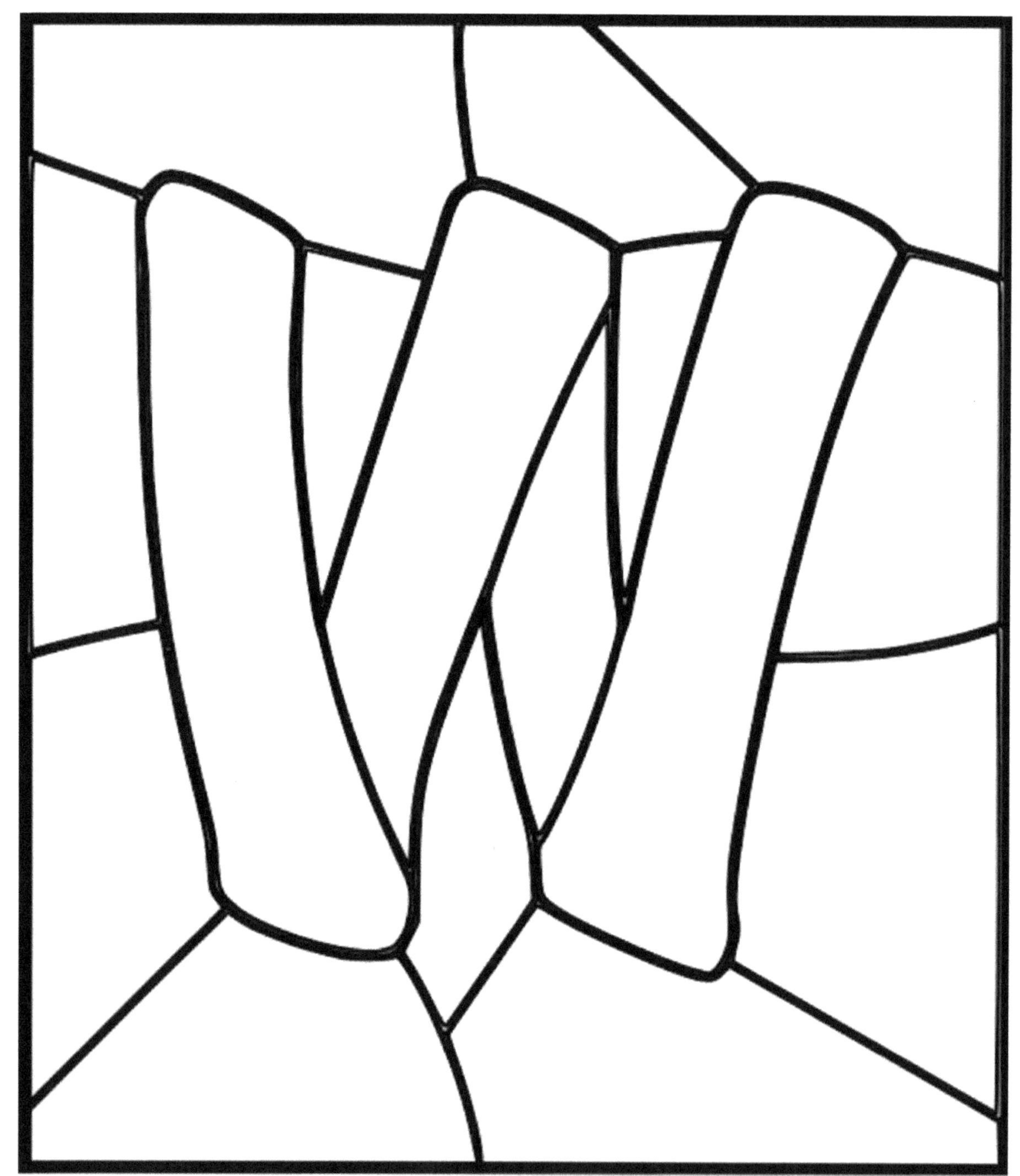

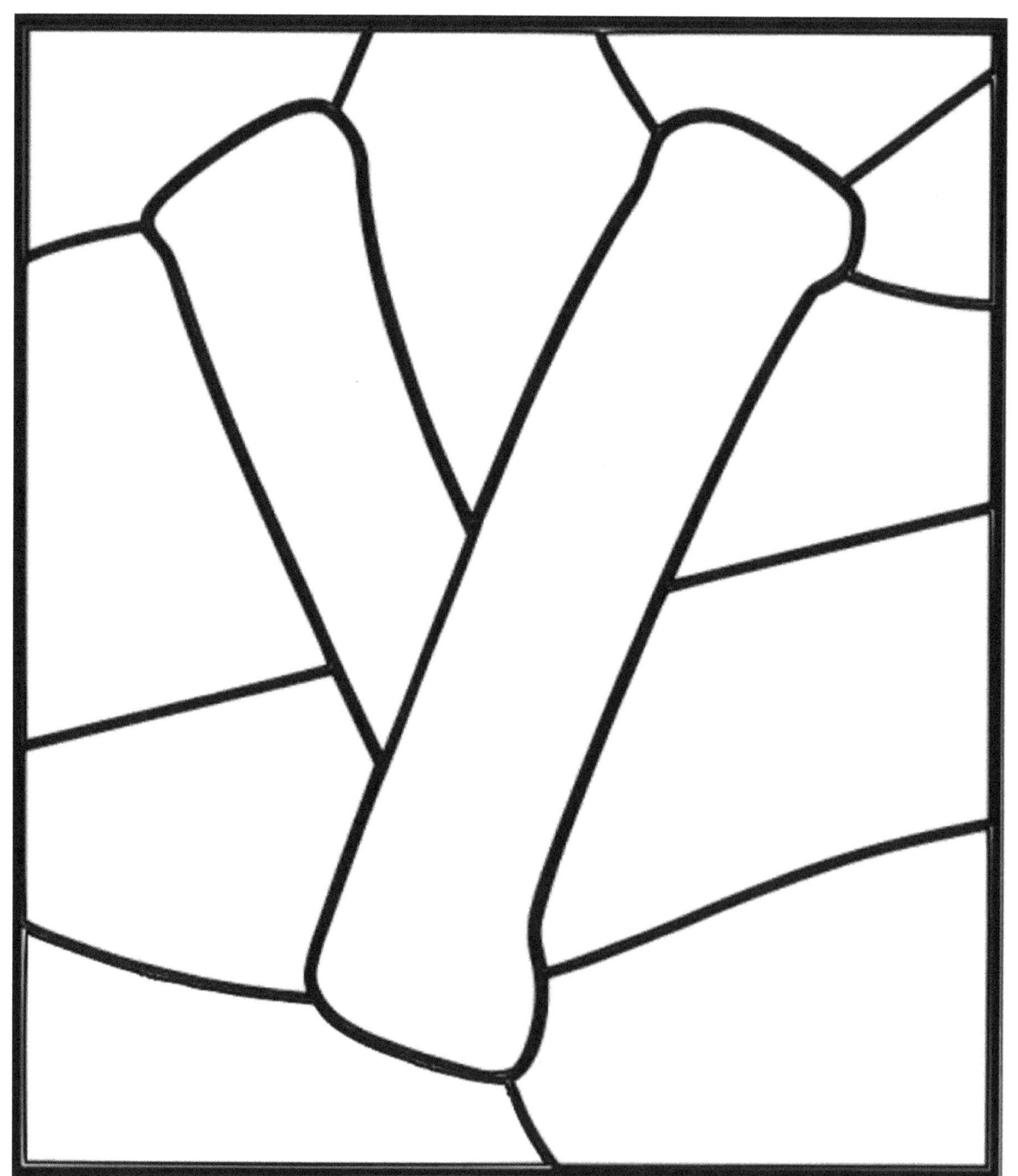

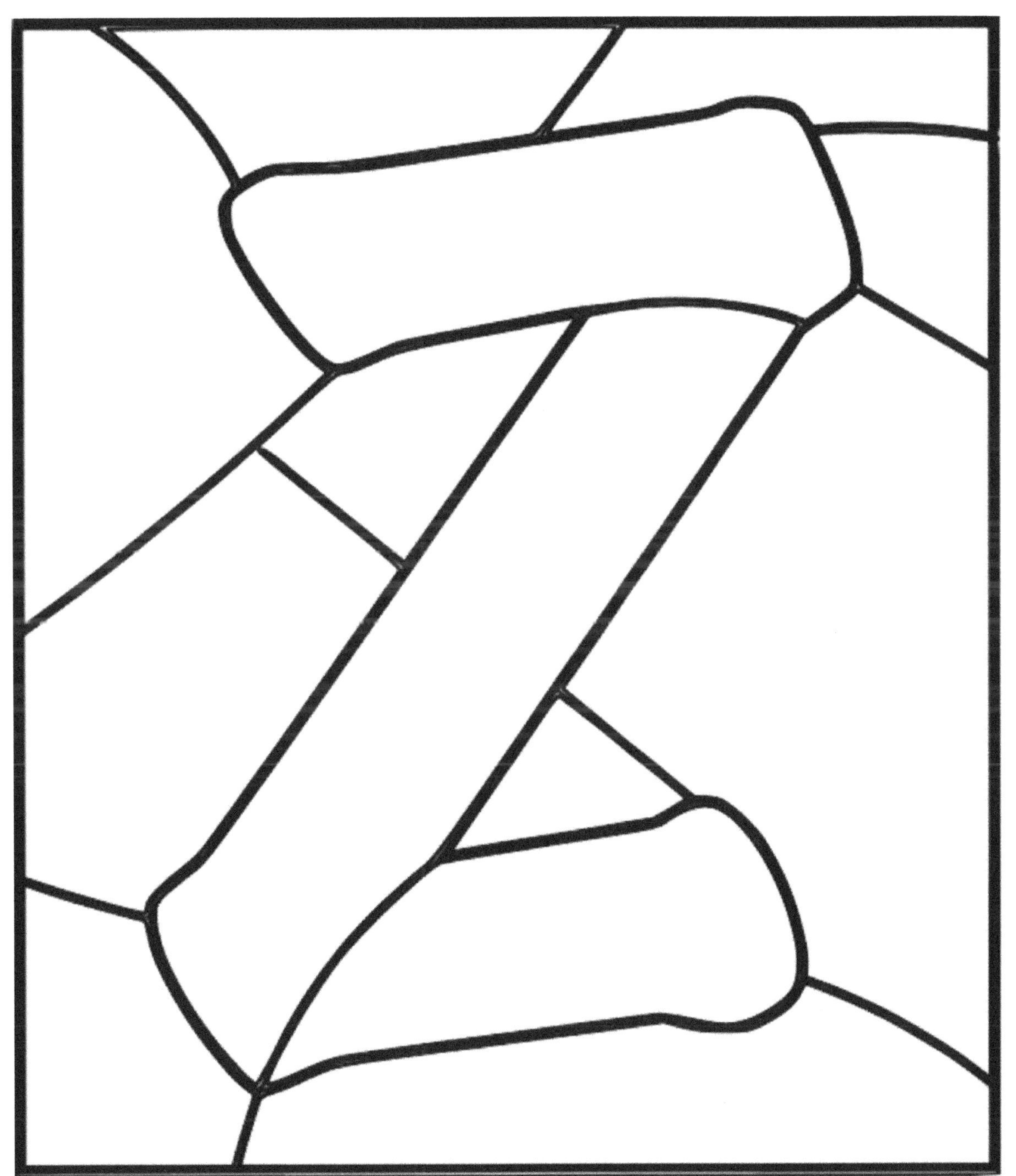

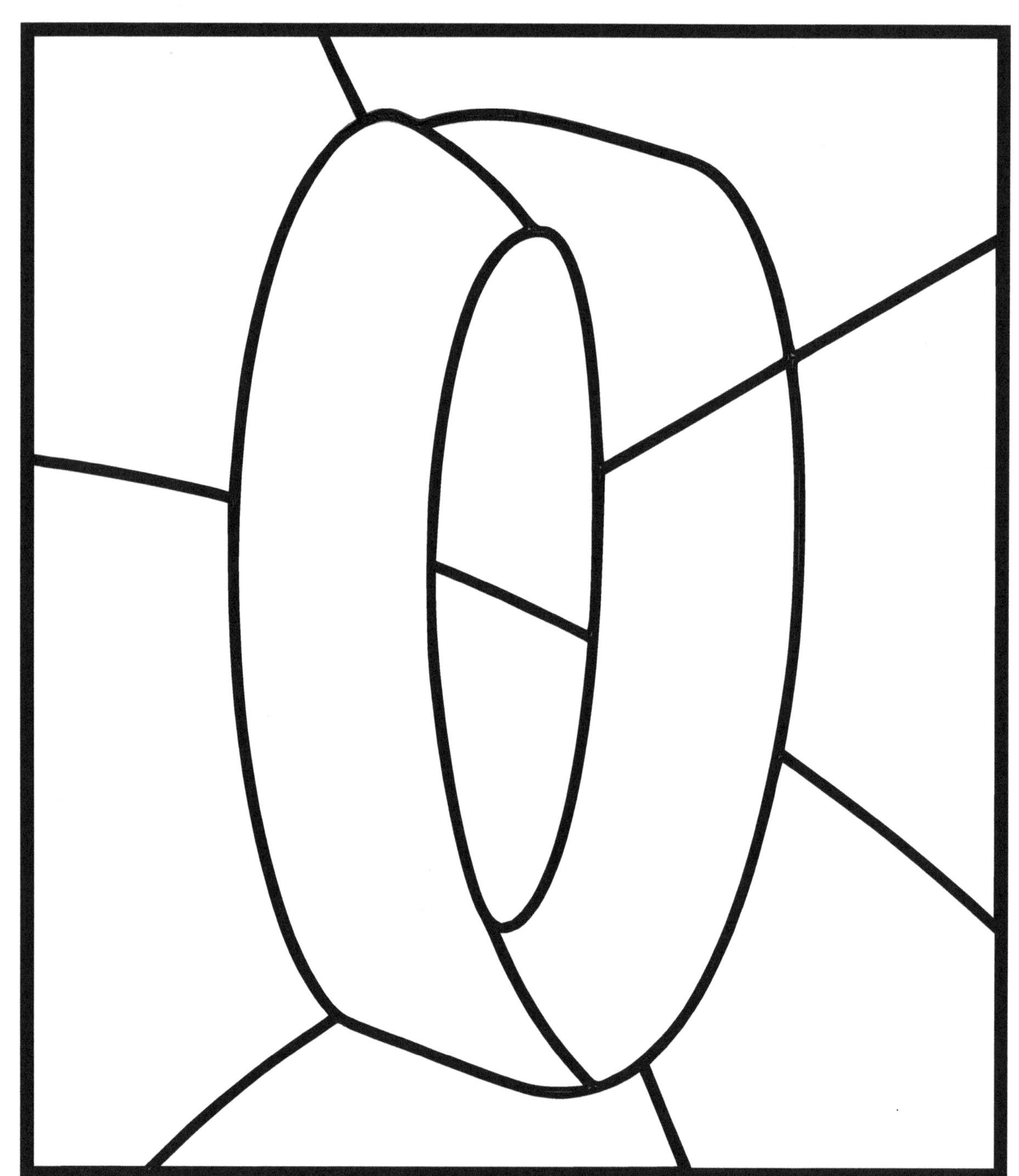

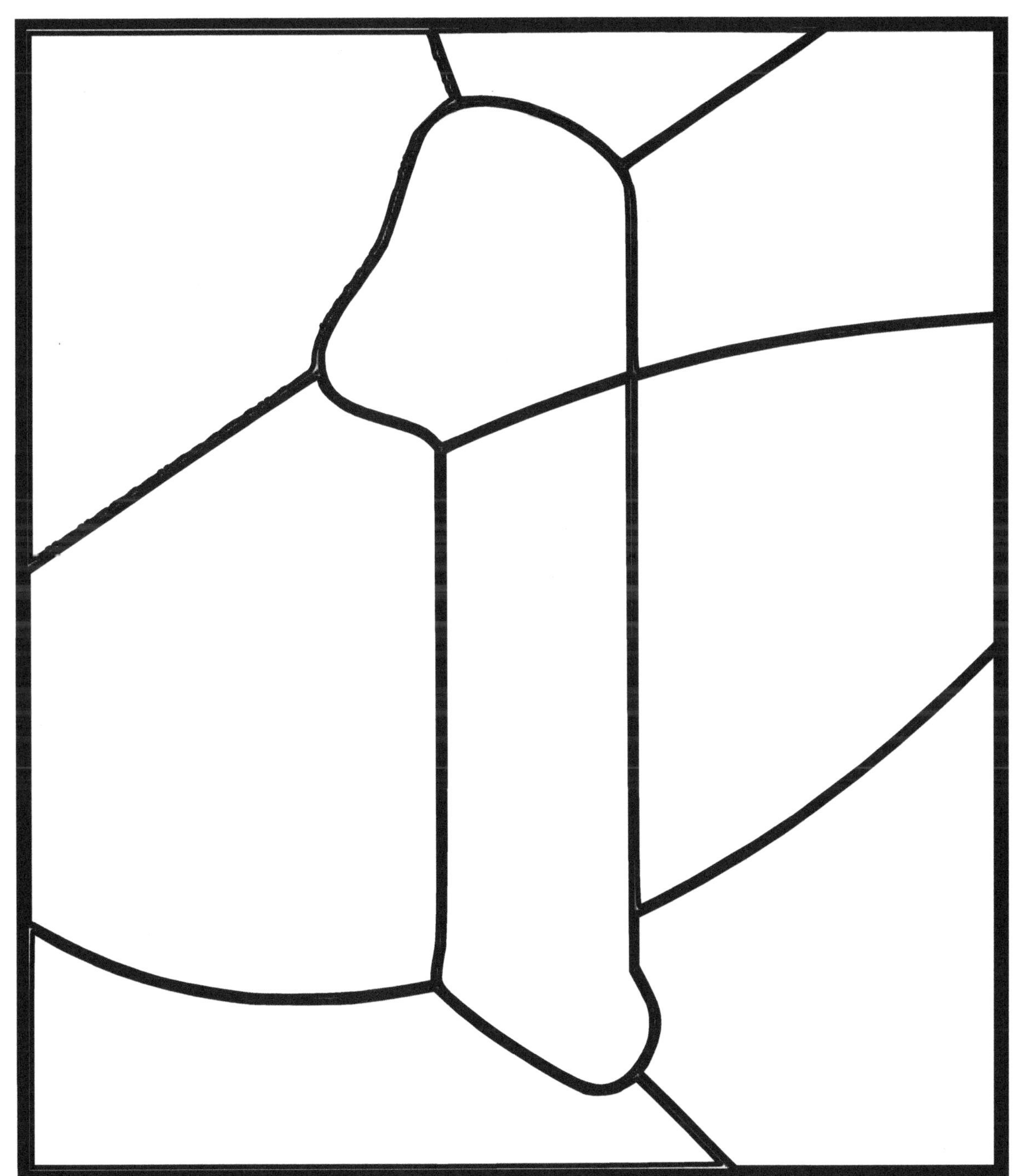

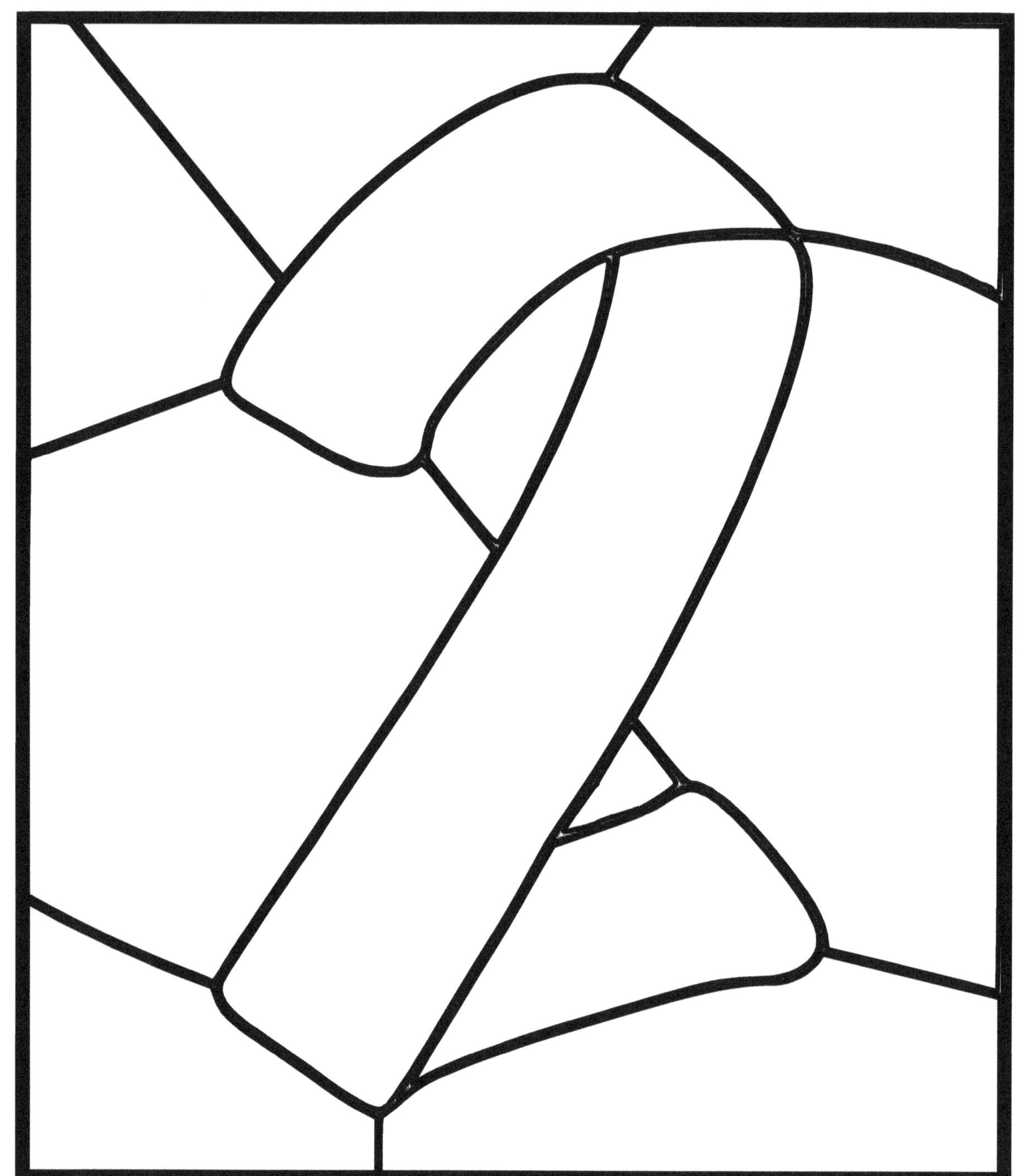

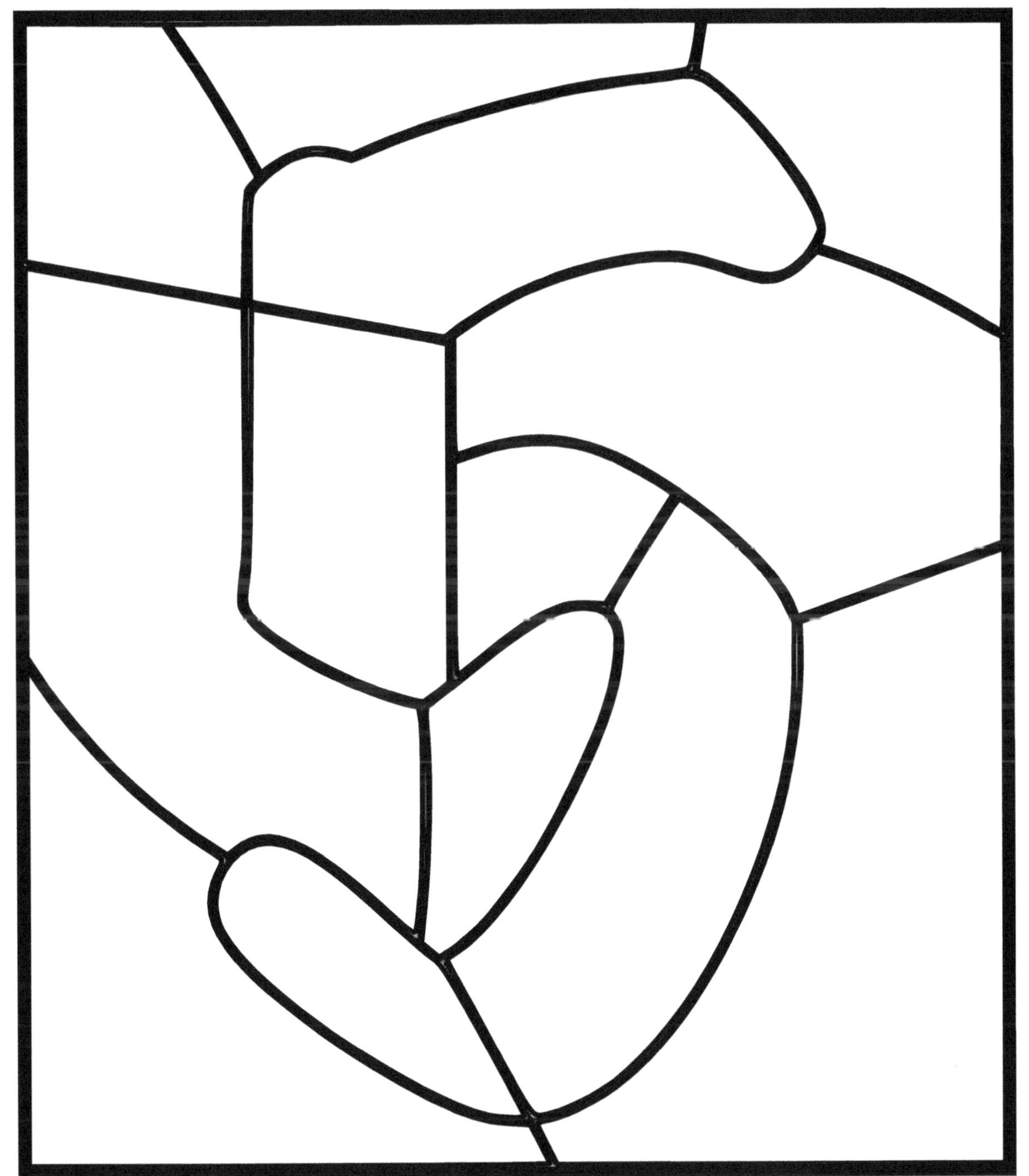

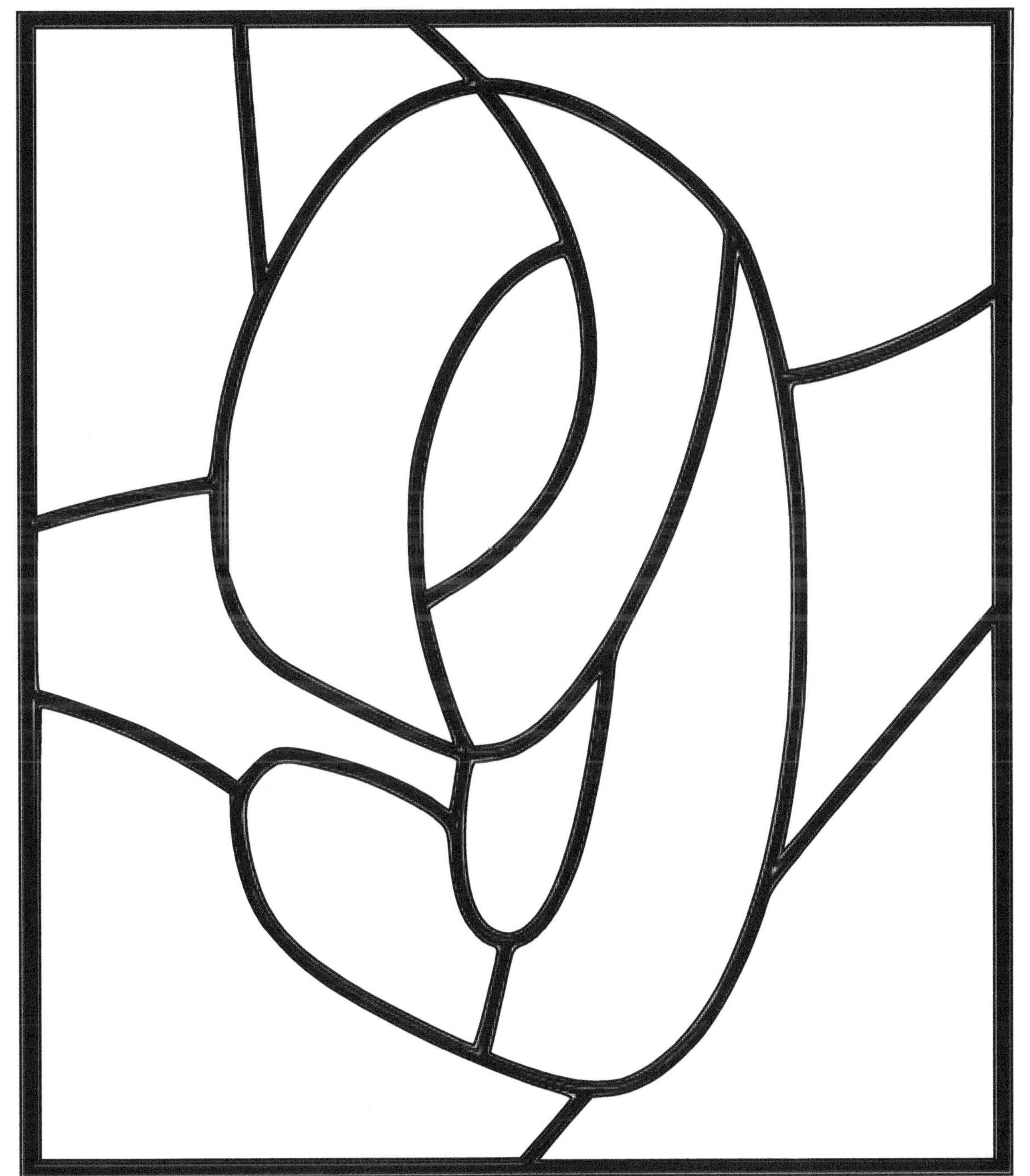

Thank you for your book purchase!
Purchase of our stained glass patterns gives full permission for unlimited retail sales of finished product or personal use and helps promote our creative efforts. If you need any assistance with our patterns for resizing, formatting or any other questions just message us.

GaryBSomers@me.com

Please don't sell actual patterns or redistribute files. Thank you!

Visit our Etsy page for more patterns!
We would love to see your creations and welcome feedback.
Leave a review with photo :)

ISBN 979-8-8692-6849-5

9 798869 268495